The Boundless Game

The Boundless Game

Soccer Stories from Across the Street to Around the World

Tim Bascom

UNIVERSITY PRESS OF KANSAS

These chapters first appeared in the following publications:
"Bishops with Balls." *Sport Literate* 16, no. 1 (Spring 2024).
"Offsides! Yankee Fans in a Premier Palace." *Writer's Workshop Review* 20 (2025).
"The Old Man and the Knee." *DSM Magazine: The Men's Book* (2011).
"Why I Can't Stop Playing Soccer." *Linden Review* 7 (May 2025).

Published by the University Press of Kansas (Lawrence, Kansas 66045), which was organized by the Kansas Board of Regents and is operated and funded by Emporia State University, Fort Hays State University, Kansas State University, Pittsburg State University, the University of Kansas, and Wichita State University.

Library of Congress Cataloging-in-Publication Data

Print LCCN: 2025041836
ISBN 9780700641024 (paperback)
ISBN 9780700641031 (epub)

British Library Cataloguing-in-Publication Data is available.
EU Authorised Representative Details: Easy Access System Europe
Mustamäe tee 50, 10621 Tallinn, Estonia | gpsr.requests@easproject.com

Printed in the United States of America

10 9 8 7 6 5 4 3 2 1

The paper used in this publication is acid free and meets the minimum requirements of the American National Standard for Permanence of Paper for Printed Library Materials Z39.48-1992.

Cover design by Karl Janssen
Photographs: Background: Natee K Jindakum/
Shutterstock.com. Globe ball: iStock.com/f9photos

This book is dedicated to soccer lovers around the globe
and especially those who have welcomed me
onto pitches in other countries, including
England, Ethiopia, Kenya, Sudan, and Swaziland.

Contents

Preface: Hmmm. Should You Read This Book? ix

1. First Tackle 1

Did You Know? Historical Origins of the Game 3

2. On Using One's Head 5

3. One for the Ages 8

Did You Know? How the Ball Evolved 14

4. Stress, Soccer, and Relief! 16

5. Up in the Air 20

Did You Know? How Soccer Got Its Goals 23

6. Soccer at All Costs? 25

7. A Toast to the Toughest! 30

Did You Know? Why All the Goal-Scoring Hullabaloo? 35

8. ¿Hablas Español? ¿Hablas Fútbol? 37

9. One Game but Many Points of View 41

Did You Know? Just How Universal Is This Game? 45

10. Offsides! Yankee Fans in a Premier Palace 47

11. Pride vs. Spirit 54

Did You Know? Pioneers of Women's Soccer 62

12. Why I Can't Stop Playing 64

13. Religion vs. Soccer 69

Did You Know? Even Bob Marley Played! 74

14. Coaching Chaos 76

15. Wonder Girl 78

Did You Know? How Referees Took Charge 82

16. No Ball? No Problem! 84

17. Out in the Open 88

Did You Know? How Indoor Soccer Began 92

18. A United Nations of Soccer—in Kansas? 94

19. The Darker Side 99

Did You Know? A Homeless World Cup 104

20. Mr. Soccer—Oumar Seck 105

21. Football to Fútbol 112

Did You Know? Why International Games are Called Caps 119

22. Building Soccer Bridges 120

23. A Family Affair 125

Did You Know? War, Soccer, and a Surprising Truce 129

24. Bishops with Balls 131

25. Reasons We Watch 137

Did You Know? Random (but Fun) Facts 140

26. Camaraderie 141

27. No Matter What! 145

Did You Know? Who Outlasted All the Others? 153

28. The Old Man and the Knee 154

Acknowledgments 157

Preface: Hmmm. Should You Read This Book?

In the early 1500s, during the reign of the Tudor King Henry VIII, soccer was still an unrefined game called "folk football," played by people whose exploits were known only to neighbors. Teams from opposite ends of a village tried to force their way into the other side's territory with a pig's bladder stuffed with straw. They kicked it and carried it and knocked each other down in a roaming brawl that did *not* appear in national news the next day. No heroes emerged, instead just a few vague descriptions of a popular but unruly game that had to be banned due to violence.

At that time, allegorical morality plays were also the rage, staged by town guilds of craftsmen or merchants, and one of the most popular featured a central character called "Everyman." Fittingly, we don't know who wrote that play. In fact, some scholars believe the story originated in medieval Holland. But here's the point: as the protagonist of this wide-ranging book about soccer, I propose that I am a sort of "everyman." My stories, although specific, are a stand-in for the multitudinous stories of ordinary, unfamous men/women/kids/people who love to watch or play the game, including you.

I am nobody in the realm of soccer—widely known as "football." I am not Messi or Mbappé. Not Christian Pulisic or Alex Morgan or Carli Lloyd. Which means you have no reason to read this book except that I am like all the other soccer lovers worldwide who can't help watching the game or pulling on cleats.

In my case, I am still lacing cleats at the age of sixty-four not because I want to grab headlines but because soccer makes me happy. And right now, in hundreds of places around the globe, others are doing the same for the same reason. They may be barefoot boys on a dirt-and-sand patch in Mogadishu or French girls from a private school in Marseille. They may be a gaggle of twenty-something lads and lasses on a beach in Cornwall, with a cliff face behind them and waves breaking yards away. Or a village team on the hot plains of southwest Nepal who just deboarded from a van and are warming up, telling a little brother to go to the river and fill a cooler with water so they will have something to drink at halftime.

All over the globe they are taking turns, including here in the US. A coed group in Des Moines is taking the field as part of a third-tier recreational league, playing under the name Clockwork Orange simply because orange jerseys were on sale. And as for me, I am regularly joining an eclectic group of internationals, including Dmitri and Anna and Xavier, who enjoy a pickup game on a high school soccer pitch near the University of Kansas.

These athletes are playing games that may seem unimportant. However, none of the games or players are *un*important. If you think about it, all the anonymous soccer players and supportive fans—several billion of us worldwide—are actually the ones who keep the ball rolling day to day, year to year. I and you, we care enough to keep soccer on the map—all over the map, really. We are the everyman or everywoman of this astounding international phenomenon. And when we are gone, there will be others who keep "kicking around," making sure that the game of soccer—football, if you prefer—stays alive.

If you relate, read on!

1
First Tackle

My personal soccer-playing story begins in 1968 at a boarding school for expatriate children in Addis Ababa, Ethiopia, where my parents send me while they start work at a mission hospital two hundred miles to the south. Lesson #1: older boys always get the ball.

Being only seven, I must watch as the ten- and twelve-year-olds choose teams on a field in front of the sprawling adobe building that serves as staff offices, dormitory, and cafeteria. I must watch as they dash up and down this field, passing and intercepting and shooting.

One recess, though, there are not enough of the big boys, so I am allowed in.

I race everywhere, chasing anyone who has the ball. I do this because I know that my teammates—all older—will never pass the ball to me.

I chase guys who dribble in circles. I stab with a foot. I swipe. But they are too quick, too long-legged and fast—until I throw my butt to the ground and thrust my sliding leg across the path of one of these dribblers, not only blocking the ball but sending him flopping.

Triumph!

I dance away with the spinning sphere, experiencing what it is like to be in possession at last. To be chased instead of chasing.

Without instruction, I have "invented" one of the most basic of defensive moves—the slide tackle. I'll use this the rest of my life. In fact, when fifty years have passed and I am very practiced at it, I'll use the same motion as a patented *offensive* move, surprising defenders by tapping the ball to the side, beyond the reach of their long legs, and then doing a sliding kick that sends the ball flying around them. It's a last-ditch move, but sometimes it works, surprising even the guy waiting back there in the goal, who was *not* expecting an actual shot.

In soccer, as in any sport, you practice until a move comes to you like second nature. You develop that move until there is no thought, just action.

The slide tackle? I own that.

DID YOU KNOW?

Historical Origins of the Game

Although the British will always claim to have invented soccer, a similar game, called Cuju, was played in China as far back as 206 BC. Players were divided into two teams of twelve to sixteen, and they couldn't use hands, instead kicking a ball into a net. Versions of this game, which evolved over centuries, were played not just by men but also by women and children, who are pictured in ancient Chinese paintings.

It actually took the Brits a millennium to come up with a medieval equivalent, and their "folk football" was much less refined than Cuju, allowing players not only to kick the stuffed pig bladder but to carry it, tackling or wrestling for control.

Over a long time, this rougher "football" became more formalized, and it shifted onto an open field, where players tried to take the ball to an object or designated area—a "goal." Then, in early-nineteenth-century England, schools began to form clubs, competing against each other and formulating rules. At first, players could still use their hands and wrestle. But in the 1840s, when some of these emerging "football" clubs adopted rules established at Rugby School, they initiated what would become modern rugby. Other schools agreed on a different set of rules, forbidding the use of hands and requiring that the ball be kicked into a framed goal, and they initiated modern soccer. The latter rules, authorized as "football association" rules, were published in 1863, drawing on regulations from Sheffield, and they included the size of the goal, the corner kick, the handball penalty, and the free kick.

Actually, the word "soccer" is tied to those original Football Association rules. People started putting together a shortened version of "association" (i.e., "socc") and a common suffix (i.e., "er"). However, with time, the English public let go of that rather abstract term and turned to "football," which made better sense. In the US, meanwhile, Americans had invented their own "football," which took away that labeling option. That is why, today, Americans still use the discarded English term "soccer" for a game that the rest of the world calls "football."

2

On Using One's Head

After five years working in Ethiopia, my missionary parents took my two brothers and me back to Kansas to live in a little town called Troy. Six years ripped by. Then they surprised us by deciding to return to Ethiopia. Once again, I found myself playing soccer on that boarding-school field at the edge of Addis Ababa, where the red, iron-rich soil peeked through thinning grass and where a towering eucalyptus near midfield almost always harbored a perched kite with others circling on knifelike wings. Now, though, I was sixteen.

An asphalt sidewalk cut across the field at the thirty-yard line. I had forgotten about that during the years in Kansas. Better not to try any slide tackles there!

The same walkway continued down a hill to classrooms where I had begun grade school. Everything still seemed familiar. However, I had missed critical years of foot-skill development while my father served as a town doctor in Kansas, and that skill gap meant I was definitely going to play defense when we took on the guys coming to scrimmage from the Norwegian School, including the legendary Lars, who could juggle a ball on his pumping knees as he ran.

Me, I couldn't even keep a ball in the air three times, juggling with feet. I had no ball control after the years away. In fact, I was still relearning how to turn my foot out when kicking instead of using the tip of my shoe. So I decided I would stay back and simply get in the way.

Having spent six years playing American football, I was wearing the wrong sort of cleats, not true soccer "boots." They were pointy and curled up at the toes, which meant I would undoubtedly be embarrassed when I tried to intercept a pass, slicing under the ball with a bent toe, then popping it straight up. I was already learning to accept such embarrassments, though. Perhaps that is why I ran around that day wearing a goofy blue, polka-dotted baseball cap—the only guy on the field who might be mistaken for a jester.

The Norwegian goalie cradled the ball after one of our failed shots. He took two steps and punted it high and long toward my side of the defensive backfield, where the sprinting Lars hoped to receive it and zip around me. I knew I could back up and prepare for his dribbling attack, but instead, I dashed toward the spot where the ball would arc down, and I removed my cap as I ran. As it turned out, I arrived just a step ahead of Lars, who crashed into me at the very moment the ball arrived, smacking the flat of my head.

My jarred brain ignited. I tasted iron. Later, I would learn that you must lead with the rim of the head, not the flat top. I would learn to even throw my forehead into the ball. But all I knew at that moment was that Lars did *not* get what he wanted. The ball bounced straight up, and when it dropped back down, one of my teammates fielded it. Then he passed it away and shouted, "Desta testa," which is Amharic for "joyful header."

Joyful indeed—this feeling of having successfully foiled the other player, of having not flinched either.

In Troy, Kansas, where no one played soccer, I had been donning shoulder pads and a helmet ever since sixth grade. As a running back, I had cracked heads with helmeted defenders, getting used to the jolt. I was not afraid of this inflated sphere even if it did drop from forty feet in the air. Soon I would know how to receive it properly. Soon I would bang it right back or direct it to a teammate.

This new skill—the header—would become a main way, as a relatively untrained defender, for me to prove my worth. It and the slide tackle would be enough of a deterrent to get me onto the second-string team at my boarding school, where I could watch and learn and—who knows?—maybe, someday, make the first string.

3
One for the Ages

On December 18, 2022, I watched what some claim to be the best game in the history of soccer, the World Cup final between Argentina and France. I watched it with my brother Nat, with whom I have played soccer for half a century, and much of the meaningfulness came from high-fiving him in the basement of his house or pogo jumping in a huddle with our wives and my soccer-playing nephew.

Just the day before—a Saturday—Nat and I had joined sixteen guys for a weekly pickup game at the old limestone stadium on the campus of Kansas State University, doing this despite the temperature being 25 degrees Fahrenheit. Although we were the oldest guys on the field—sixty-one and fifty-eight years old—we triumphed with a team that included two other oldies in their forties and fifties. I even scored three goals, a rare hat trick. And Nat teased two of our young opponents, Korean college students, asking them what they expected given that he and I and the other two soccer "elders" had a combined 170 years of experience.

What I'm trying to say is that when you've spent your whole life playing soccer with a family member—becoming an effective defensive tag team and taking turns sending each other up to play offense—and when you have won rec-league tournaments together and juggled with your sons in the parking lot and shared cleats and tried to encourage each other through injured hamstrings, twisted ankles, bruised hips, jammed toes, gashed shins, tweaked knees, and smacked foreheads, then you have an especially strong, amplified response to watching a game like this World Cup final—between not just two nations with well-established soccer traditions but two of the most admired players of all time: the young twenty-three-year-old Mbappé and the aging thirty-six-year-old Lionel Messi.

I did not expect Argentina to win, given how incredibly gifted the French team had appeared to be during early games—especially Mbappe and his teammate Giroud, who both were competing with Messi for the Golden Boot, an honor given to the highest scorer at each World Cup. Mbappé, with his instantaneous bursts of unpredictable dribbling, and Giroud, with his fierce, will-not-be-denied headers, seemed unbeatable, especially since they had a deep bench of standout players to support them.

However, Argentina stormed the French from the opening whistle, playing with inspired grit while making single-touch passes that seemed so quick and exact that they might have been preordained. They flicked the ball to each other as if they were in each others' brains. They played as if they had become a single hypercoordinated entity, a soccer-playing hive.

And Messi? Oh, my Lord! What clever and perfect dribbling. What relentless running, punctuated by slicing, looping, side-tapping passes or bullet-like shots. Over and over, he spun out of the clutch of three or four defenders. Not just that—he raced back to play defense, outhustling bigger opponents and bumping them off the ball or keeping them from the headers they wanted even though he was half a foot shorter. In the first half alone, Messi must have touched the ball thirty times, while poor Mbappé, shackled to the left front corner of the field and a goal-scoring fixation, had literally touched the ball three times.

Argentina scored on a penalty kick by Messi after a teammate was tripped in the penalty zone. Then Argentina scored again, creating the most beautiful sequence of passes that I had seen since the World Cup had begun a month earlier, when there were thirty-two teams, then sixteen, then eight, then four, then only two. From one end of the field to the other, the Argentinean players stitched the ball through the French defenders, ending with a breakaway player who, instead of taking the expected shot, made one last generous pass to a winger streaking in from the side. The final single-touch shot zipped right over the sliding goalie and into the corner of the net, and I was in love, not just with one superstar—Messi—but with a full team, a wonderful conglomeration of guys who were creatively melding themselves into something greater than any individual.

As a player with modest skills, I have always been drawn to teams that play a unified and generous game—not relying on just one or two razzle-dazzle stars. My brother also loves teams that play "team ball." When we play pickup games, we insist on playing for the same side, quoting the Psalms to make our case—"Behold, how good and how pleasant it is for brethren to dwell together in unity!"

What we were seeing that day in the basement of Nat's house was that, yes, Messi was the heartbeat of this Argentinean group, but he was the heartbeat of a very shared spirit. Without his unselfish, radar-like accuracy on a midfield pass that split two approaching defenders, that remarkable sequence of passes would never have occurred and Argentina would never have scored its second goal.

So now, if I was in love with Messi, I was in love because he basically symbolized the collective spirit of the whole team. I was joining the 75 percent of the world who were already rooting for Messi to receive the crowning glory of a World Cup trophy, but I was joining because of his generosity.

Here, on the biggest stage imaginable, with nearly 1.5 billion viewers, Messi was demonstrating that he was much, much more than a goal-hoarding glorymonger. Unlike pouting Ronaldo from

Portugal, who had been sent to the bench for his last World Cup game because he was so selfish and divisive, Messi was as likely to assist a shot as to take it. And he would come back to help steal the ball, setting up other players.

At halftime, the game looked properly sealed, moving toward its rightful destiny. I was ready for Argentina to ease up, withdrawing into a defensive posture and maintaining the 2-point lead, maybe even conceding a goal. So I was not at all prepared for the drama that ensued—first a successful penalty kick by Mbappé and then, only a minute and thirty seconds later, a dagger that Mbappé pulled out of the air and sent hurling past the Argentinean goalie to tie the score.

I could write pages about the anguish we felt down in that basement, and the rising desperation as the French began to pound on Argentina's door during injury time. I could describe, for instance, the goalie making a body-sacrificing, sprawling save to barely keep Argentina in the game.

I could also write about the ecstatic euphoria when, having gone into overtime, Messi and his teammates penetrated the French defense and smacked a deflected shot, then smacked it again, somehow knocking the reluctant ball past the goal line, where a French defender—too late—slid in a desperate attempt to block it.

How we screamed when that overtime goal was confirmed on replay, all of it happening with such pinball rapidity that we needed a minute to realize that it was actually Messi who had made the final, quicksilver jab to put the ball over the line. That desperate ricochet goal, scored in overtime, suddenly lifted him over Mbappé for the Golden Boot, which made us cheer even more. What a wonderful bonus.

By that point, it was clear that this game was one of the most remarkable in all soccer history. But incredibly, the contest was still not done. To our chagrin, Mbappé outjuked a set of defenders just a few minutes later, then fired so suddenly that a startled Argentinean could not get his elbow out of the way, which led to a second Mbappé penalty kick, tying the game and flipping the Golden Boot right back to Mbappé.

The wheel of fate was turning inexorably, grinding and screeching, and that basement in Kansas filled with sad groans and thrust-out hands as we stared in shock. Another ten minutes passed with nothing decided. Another ten minutes of tense stalemate. And we could not believe that it had to end this way. Still tied after overtime? And now a penalty shootout?

For a few seconds, my brother got right down on the floor and hid his face behind a cloth-covered footstool, not sure he could bear the torture of watching the final ten kicks. My wife left the room and took her blood-pressure pill. I stood and paced.

What a stupendous situation—to have the two greatest scorers of the tournament start the series of penalty kicks, each hammering home another goal for their nation. It was as if the soccer gods had scripted it, as if this game had been written by Homer or Virgil. I feared tragedy, of course. But when the Argentinean goalie guessed where the second French shooter would shoot, slapping the ball away, we screamed and danced and whacked each other's hands, along with the vast majority of those 1.5 billion viewers who agreed that this game should—rightfully—go to the stronger of the two teams.

The second Argentinean kicker made his shot. Then the Argentinean goalie dove the right direction once more, psyching out the third French kicker so that he shot wide, and we burst with cathartic joy because now, now, now it seemed that the gods would truly honor the wishes of us all.

When the fourth kicker took his place for Argentina, we stopped breathing. He walked away from the ball, turned, contemplated the climactic moment. He took three or four accelerating steps, and we all leaned forward. Then what joy as he drilled the ball right past the French goalie into the net. He, of course, tore his shirt off and raced into the history books. With five goals to three, the last French shooter had no reason to even take a shot. Game over!

Down there in that Kansas basement, even the dog danced, infected by our enthusiastic yells. And thousands of miles away, in Buenos Aires, a million singing pedestrians surged into the streets, spontaneously jogging toward the obelisk at the center of the city. Not a car could move, but drivers didn't care. They sat and pressed their horns, or they parked and joined the human torrent. They were such a huge mass that they could be seen on satellite photos—so loud that, who knows, maybe they could even be heard out there in space.

It was a party to end all parties, and we joined in with all the joyous Argentineans for just a few earth-stopping moments in a solidarity that is so rare that it seems immeasurably precious. Nat and I—who take great pleasure from moments when we, as brothers, stop attackers in a combined pincer movement, then get the ball moving back downfield with a couple coordinated passes—roared our affirmation, slapping hands together in old-school style.

In an era when the media focuses so much attention on individual players, ignoring those who don't have a personal "brand," it was a delight to see a team winning on team play. Clubs with lots of money can purchase superstars, guaranteeing more wins, but at the World Cup, where players step away from clubs to play for their nation, they either unite selflessly or stay splintered by personal aspirations. What a delight, then, to see a star meld into his team, energizing them with his own generous approach. What a delight to see the group triumph!

C'est la vie, Mbappé. C'est la vie.

DID YOU KNOW?
How the Ball Evolved

Until the mid-1800s, soccer balls were still being made from a pig's bladder—although they could be inflated instead of being stuffed with feathers or straw, and they were protected by a hand-stitched leather casing.

Despite such improvements, the nineteenth-century balls were not uniform in size or shape. They flew and bounced unpredictably. The pig bladders wore out quickly too, not lasting more than a few games.

Then, in 1855, the American entrepreneur Charles Goodyear invented a way to harden and shape rubber. He began to produce rubber balls that were rounder and more uniform in size. Soon after, H. J. Lindon figured out how to create rubber bladders that could be inflated, and these new bladders were much more durable and consistent in shape, making the ball fly more truly. The only problem was that they still needed a leather casing, and that casing had a laced opening for inflating the bladder. As a result of the lacings, the new balls were heavier to one side. As they spun through the air, they wobbled or dipped, which drove goalies crazy.

Frustrated by erratic shots, a goalie from Denmark finally decided to experiment with materials, and that goalie—Eigel

Nielsen—can be thanked for the basic design that manufacturers still rely on today. Nielsen began a sports supply company called Select, and in 1951, Select introduced an integral valve, getting rid of the old-fashioned external lacing. The ball stayed inflated longer, was more balanced, and no longer made headers painful due to a laced ridge!

A few more years, and Nielsen's company introduced an iconic outer casing as well. Designed by the famous architect Richard Buckminster Fuller, the new outer layer was influenced by his work on geodesic domes; thus, it had twenty hexagonal panels of leather and twelve pentagonal sections stitched together.

Fuller's geodesic ball went on the market in 1962, and Adidas helped to make the design iconic at the 1970 World Cup in Mexico. The new look was named Telstar in homage to a satellite that had recently been launched with alternating black-and-white panels. Like that satellite, the Telstar soccer ball has carried us right into the future.

4
Stress, Soccer, and Relief!

Did I tell you that when we went back to Ethiopia in the seventies, we arrived at the height of the Marxist revolution that had overthrown Emperor Haile Selassie? Or that I could count gunshots every night out there on the streets of Addis Ababa, just beyond the fence of my school?

Counterrevolutionaries were ambushing and assassinating government leaders, while military agents were making nighttime raids, shooting so-called enemies of the state, then leaving their bodies on the curb. One afternoon when I was walking with my girlfriend beside the school soccer pitch, machine-gun bursts broke out and kept crackling for so long that all of us ran for the cafeteria. Not until a day later did we learn the cause. Over one hundred college and high school students had been gunned down by the military to stop a protest against the brutal tactics of Colonel Mengistu and his ruling "Committee of Equals."

During those days of unpredictable violence, the main boulevard in Addis was plastered with red posters of an Ethiopian peasant strangling Uncle Sam, along with the bold slogan "Go Home Yankee." Maybe we really *should* have gone home—back to Troy, Kansas—but my parents kept working at their mountaintop clinic until the last possible day, when the mission director realized the clinic could be seized by local cadres, leading to house arrest. He sent a single-engine Cessna to fly my parents out, telling them to burn every record of connection to local patients or church workers.

During the months that followed, my parents actually *did* consider taking us back to America, but they decided to follow a diaspora of other missionaries headed to Kenya, where they would wait until restationed. That meant my brother Nat and I had to start over at a new boarding school an hour west of Nairobi, on the edge of the great Rift Valley.

Soccer, through all this, was a way to release stress, to be reminded that "normal life" was still possible. In Addis, if I jumped into a pickup game, I didn't have to think about posters of Uncle Sam being strangled or teenage protesters being gunned down. I could concentrate on the spinning ball. And when I had to start over at Rift Valley Academy in Kenya, I was thankful for soccer again because it gave me a way out of the natural worries that went with being in yet another new community with dozens of strangers.

Out there on the soccer pitch, I had a way to ease into conversation, talking to guys I might never have greeted otherwise. A short, tough-looking fullback with the nickname "Porky" didn't seem a likely friend. He had so much blond hair on his arms and legs that he glowed when the sun got low on the horizon. But he welcomed me during practice, asking what life had been like back in Addis Ababa.

The same was true for cool-cat Dave, who was already sporting a beard. I didn't expect attention, let alone kindness, from a guy who wore a denim vest and swaggered around like John Travolta in the show *Welcome Back, Kotter.* But he too opened the door into this new home.

We played most of our matches at home but sometimes traveled away during that junior year at Rift Valley Academy. Typically, that meant taking a bus to one of the elite Kenyan boarding schools like Lenana, in Nairobi. But I remember one game in particular because we had to travel farther, to a poor school in the town of Machakos, where the soccer pitch doubled as a cattle pasture. That cockeyed grassy meadow was dotted with cow pies. The goalposts had no nets, and they were made from wooden poles nailed together. The field had never been leveled, so it slumped to one corner. In fact, when I got down in a little valley to the right side of our goal, I could not even see the other goal.

A humble game, yes. However, there was something wonderfully zany and freeing about running around in such an undeveloped natural setting—with a local boy switching a humpbacked ox to keep it off the field and my friends grimacing if the ball skipped through a splat of manure. To play like that was to be out in the real world, not retreating to an idyllic set-apart space. In some odd way, it bonded me more fully to humanity as a whole.

Eventually my parents got visas into Sudan and were allowed out of the purgatory of moving from one mission guesthouse to another. They flew into Khartoum, then traveled hundreds of miles south and east to a station near the Ethiopian border, where they were charged with reviving a tin-roofed adobe hospital that had been abandoned during the Sudanese civil war of the sixties.

After a while, my older brother, John, came to join my parents, taking a break from college; then my brother Nat and I arrived on holiday. Being active took extra willpower in the blazing new setting, where heavy-limbed baobabs loomed overhead, leafless in the scorching heat, and where the whole community settled into a silent stupor in the midafternoon. Sometimes, though, when the sun was low on the horizon, my brothers and I rode bikes down a dirt path to the ramshackle village of Doro and played soccer with a group of men and boys who gathered on a dusty square outside the only shop, a sweltering adobe-and-tin room that had a few cans of food for sale, a few bottles of hot Fanta, and warm pita bread straight from a brick kiln.

Even at dusk, that flat, dirt-baked field in Doro felt like an extension of the baker's kiln—easily over 100 degrees. Any slide tackle or fall left me with a film of brown powder that turned to sweaty mud.

There was only one true ball in the village, and it was repeatedly in need of repair, with a rubber bladder that had inner-tube patches glued onto it. The panels of the leather casing had been restitched, and the ball wasn't weighted evenly, so it wobbled as it rolled, but it served its purpose. Once again, soccer gave me a way to come out of my shell and get to know some people from a new community feeling less intimidated by their foreign appearance or their unfamiliar mix of Arabic and Mabaan.

After a while, we brought our less battered ball from the mission station, lending it for games, which meant we were even more welcome. Older men would stop to watch in their white, gown-like jalabiyas. They laughed to see such pale strange boys playing with the locals, but their laughter was not derisive, and we came back regularly.

Here too soccer was a way to let go of the worries and frustrations that went with a new way of life: neighborhood pigs that crowded under our eaves to grunt and squeal, a passing leper who wanted to shake my hand, scorpions scuttling under the dining room table, bats careening around the bedroom.

All those "problems" faded with a rolling ball and people running. My own instinctive movements pushed aside cerebral cares. And even when I could not understand the shouts of the boys and men as they passed or chased, I felt like I was in relationship to them, able to appreciate the occasional cheer or laugh. Together, we shared a physical understanding that was unique to this game yet universal. In a way, we had begun to speak a shared language.

5

Up in the Air

At that remote home in Sudan, my brothers and I juggled the ball often, passing it back and forth from feet to knees to heads. We juggled in the cooler hours of the morning or late in the afternoon when the sun had come down from its searing zenith. We juggled on the cement floor in the stark, tin-roofed living room—until Mom shooed us outside. Then we juggled on the bare brown ground, sweating as the neighbor's pigs watched from under the eaves.

We took that practice ball everywhere—whether walking down to the hospital or getting out of the Land Rover to fill barrels at the hand-pumped well. In fact, we once even took it onto a vintage DC-3 for a flight to the Nile.

That sixty-foot-long, two-prop plane had been leased by the mission to deliver grain to villages suffering from drought. Designed for World War II paratroopers, it still had canvas bucket seats down the sides, facing the middle, but on this particular occasion, the aisle between the bucket seats was stacked with bulky bags of grain meant to bring famine relief.

We flew first to the town of Renk, near the Nile, where the pilots, two British expats, intended to launch multiple flights. However, when we landed on the dirt airstrip, the overloaded plane got stuck in a mudhole caused by a recent rainstorm. We had to climb off and unload dozens of the 150-pound burlap bags, then gather twenty local men to help push the plane onto a drier part of the strip.

Seeing that the rainy season might be starting, the British pilots were spooked now. Afraid of their plane being stranded on swampy land, they reneged on the whole grain-delivery plan, insisting they had to fly back to Khartoum. As a result, our family was split in half, with only my father and older brother staying to dive-bomb villages in a smaller, single-engine plane, dropping one bag at a time. My brother Nat and I had to travel to Khartoum instead, since we would fly from there back to boarding school in Kenya.

Frustrated, I stared out the window behind my bucket seat as the DC-3 rumbled down the bumpy airstrip and lifted into the air, sweeping over the silver ribbon of the Nile. I was upset by the separation of our family, and I was upset because I had looked forward to the adventure of delivering grain to needy villagers.

However, after I unbuckled my seatbelt and stood, I couldn't help but be intrigued by the open corridor of the now empty fuselage. As we growled through the sky, ten thousand feet above the vast brown landscape, I remembered our soccer ball in the luggage rack. With no passengers to bother and no stewardess to scold, why not have some fun?

Our amused mother waved from her bucket seat as Nat and I began to make little passes on the slick aluminum floor, then stepped back for longer passes. After we had gained confidence, we tipped the ball into the air with our toes, juggling it while jogging in place. We tapped it back and forth, keeping it aloft ten, fifteen, twenty times, and we laughed with delight at the paradox of keeping an object in the air while the whole plane itself was in the air.

Since that afternoon high over the Nile in 1978, I've kicked a soccer ball lots of places. I've played a rapid-fire game of three-on-three inside a racquetball court. I've played a curving game of six-on-six at a baseball diamond in Iowa, using a section of chain link behind first base for a goal. I've also played on a pristine snow-covered lawn in the Rocky Mountains, where the thin air burned my lungs and the ball thunked down, then stuck. But that experience of juggling a ball in a DC-3 stays with me most vividly.

I'll never forget the response of the ruddy, bearded copilot when he heard Nat and me hooting and glanced back through the open cockpit door. He grinned widely. Then he put out a fist and lifted a thumb.

Clearly, soccer was something to enjoy anywhere.

DID YOU KNOW?

How Soccer Got Its Goals

The first soccer "goals" may have been the gates of two English forts in 1681, where the king's servants played a match of "football" against the servants of the duke of Albemarle. But by the 1800s, when the game had become more refined and widespread, football clubs began to set up their own makeshift goals. At first, two poles were driven into the ground. Then a string was added to avoid arguments about high balls that might or might not have passed through the area above the sticks.

That flimsy cross-string was eventually replaced by ribbon-like tape or rope, and in 1863 the side posts became permanent as the goal's dimensions were mandated by the English Football Association—eight yards wide and seven feet high. Posts were not only fixed in the ground but made of uniform four-by-four-square wood. A solid crossbar was attached as well.

Nevertheless, debates still broke out about whether a ball had truly passed between the posts and under the bar because there was still no net to guarantee where the ball had gone. According to some scholars, the net wasn't added until 1891, when an engineer in Liverpool realized he could be assured his coins were safe because they stayed in his pocket, which led him to invent a giant "pocket" for the goals at Nottingham. This invention took hold so quickly that the Football Association regulated it within a year, in time for the FA Cup Final of 1892. And there you have it: the modern soccer goal.

6

Soccer at All Costs?

As much as I love soccer, I could live without it. After all, it doesn't anchor Maslow's hierarchy of human needs. It's not as necessary as food or shelter. But for some players, it seems that fundamental.

I'm thinking particularly of Afghan players. When the US military pulled out of Afghanistan, hordes of distressed Afghans tried to force their way onto the transport planes, and a seventeen-year-old boy fell after clinging to a plane that was taking off. He dropped hundreds of feet onto the concrete airstrip, dying instantly. Zaki Anwari was his name, and he was a member of the Afghan National Youth team—a team that he knew would be disbanded by the Taliban or purged of players deemed too liberal or too tainted by American thinking.

I'm sure there was more to his attempted escape than just soccer, but since soccer was a core passion for Zaki, it must have been a major factor—enough that he would ignore his mother's pleas, close the call on his cell phone, dodge through the running crowd, and leap onto the housing of the landing gear as the plane gathered speed. He would start a new life, he believed—one in which he could freely play the game he loved. Whatever it took, he would become what he was meant to be.

Terrible. A life erased. A talented athlete with a whole future in front of him, simply gone. Today, he remains a disturbing and very important symbol of the many, many others in Afghanistan who felt the same desperation, risking everything to find a way out—plus the ones who were erased without our knowing. But what many don't realize is that the distraught throng of would-be emigrants at the Kabul International Airport also included a number of women soccer players who, like Zaki, simply could not give up the game.

In the years leading to the American pullout and the return of the Taliban regime, women had experienced increased freedom in Afghanistan. They had not only been allowed to go to school and hold jobs, but for the first time, they were allowed to play organized soccer in public. In fact, within the twenty years of US occupation, they had progressed so far that they had formed a national women's team that competed at the top level, acknowledged by FIFA.

Their captain, Khalida Popal, had weathered it all. During the era of Taliban domination, she and other teenage girls would play clandestine games in utter silence to avoid being heard by religious enforcers. Even after the American occupation brought freedom to play openly, Khalida received death threats and had to move to Denmark for safety. Nonetheless, she remained an outspoken champion for women's soccer in Afghanistan.

Imagine her horror when the Taliban swept back into Kabul and reversed the clock of history, taking away all the rights that had been established for women. Even from her distant post in Denmark, she received firsthand reports of athletes donning burkas and hiding as Taliban militia went house-to-house, trying to flush out dissidents. She sent a flurry of text messages telling players to get rid of their social media accounts, to burn their soccer kits and bury their trophies.

As a founder and first captain of the women's national team, she found that this hurt terribly. "For so long," she said, "I have been fighting to bring visibility to women of Afghanistan. . . . Now I'm telling them to silence that voice, to not talk, to not meet people, to take everything down, to remove their identities. That is very painful."

Of course, for the players actually going through this loss of identity, the impact was more devastating. The goalkeeper for the national team, who still uses the pseudonym Fati to protect her family members against retaliation, said, "I thought there was no chance for living, no chance for me to go outside again and fight for my rights. No school, no media, no athletes, nothing. We were like dead bodies in our homes."

For Fati and her teammates to live without soccer was, as she put it, a kind of death. They all knew it would stay that way as long as they remained in Afghanistan. And so began one of the most dramatic escape stories of the twenty-first century. With the help of a former American marine named Haley Carter, who had played in the US National Women's Soccer League and had served for two years as assistant coach for the Afghan women's national team, the players, although scattered and hiding, began to organize. Carter, who used her marine connections to prepare a possible evacuation, told them to pack single backpacks, including food and water. They were instructed to charge their phones and take turns using them to save battery power. They donned burkas before leaving their houses. Then they converged at the Kabul airport.

A number of the players had written Carter's cell number on their arms in case their phones were confiscated, and they had steeled themselves for the harassment sure to come. Fati, in defiance of the repression, wore her official soccer shorts under the burka, even though she risked discovery as she was kicked and hit with rifle butts while trying to reach the airport gates. When the women finally broke through, they were greatly relieved, then equally crestfallen. The marine sentry whom they approached had not been briefed about the secret password set up by Carter in Houston, and he refused them entry.

The women called Carter, panicking, but she was not able to reverse the situation, urging them to hold on as she reached out to other connections in the military. Not sure what to do, the group finally turned and tried to reach a different gate, hoping to meet a guard who would be more aware of their situation. Somehow, they slipped by another Taliban security detail, and when they raced toward several Australian soldiers after forty-eight grueling hours of harassment and denial, those soldiers understood their shouts about being from the national women's soccer team. To their amazement, the whole group was allowed through.

Almost instantly, the young women boarded an immense cargo plane with no windows. They sat willy-nilly on the hard metal floor, relieved but also saddened, as it took off. They realized they would probably never see their home country again.

Exhausted, they fell asleep on each other's shoulders. And when they finally deboarded hours and hours later, they found that they were in a country they had probably never imagined visiting, let alone making it their home: Australia.

Most of those women soccer players are still in Australia today, still hoping to recover their dream as members of the Afghan women's national team. A Melbourne club has given them practicing privileges. They have a coach and play in an Australian league. They have team uniforms again. However, those uniforms feature only numbers, no family names, since they must protect mothers, fathers, and siblings from possible Taliban persecution. And there is no national name on their jerseys because their nation refuses to acknowledge that they exist.

Having experienced a violent revolution myself, I can relate somewhat. Checkpoints and AK-47s are distantly familiar from my youth in Ethiopia. But I didn't go through those hazards as a female, nor was I told I could never again use the hard-earned skills that gave me my greatest pleasure.

So what can I do except applaud the courage and determination of women like Fati, who insisted, even after all the traumas of her radical decision, "We have each other. We will play together or individually. We are already a family, and no one can change it"?

A year after fleeing Afghanistan, Fati still claimed that the women who had escaped would find their way onto the international soccer stage. They would aim to make the national team of Australia or some other country that welcomed them. She vowed, "Still we are Afghans and, somehow, we will be the representatives of our nationality."

For some, playing soccer is just that crucial.

7
A Toast to the Toughest!

The one soccer position I have never wanted to play is the one position that nine out of ten players—no, ten out of eleven—don't want to play.

You guessed it! Goalkeeper.

Why, I wonder, would anyone want to play keeper? During practices, you are pulled aside to work on skills that none of your teammates need, which means that you are always learning alone—diving to snag line drives, leaping to pull down high kicks, scooping low rollers, smothering cannonballs, palming them as you stand, bowling them underhand, or holding them out in front of you so that you can take a step and punt them away.

In games too, you must stand by yourself, stranded for ninety minutes on your own little island yet expected to dive into action even if you haven't moved for prolonged periods. You wait and watch, not unlike a spectator. You can't sprint away the nervousness because you are tethered to one small space.

When it comes down to it, if you are the goalie, you are going to feel at times like you are hardly involved. The rest of the team turn their backs on you, barely aware that you are doing that little back-and-forth jig in the goal mouth, trying to stay limber. You can jog around the goalpost and grab a water bottle. They won't know. You can even lie down in the goal, and they won't know.

Practically the only time you really loom into their awareness is when you feel threatened and start yelling because one of your defenders has neglected to cover a sneaky striker or because they all need to line up more tightly, shoulder to shoulder, during a free kick, shifting their combined wall to protect a corner of the net. And when at last you have made the critical save, taking possession of the ball, what do you do? You shout at them to move away, to get back downfield, to spread out because you are going to let it rip, kicking the damn thing as far away from the goal as you can possibly manage, which means leaving yourself all alone again!

Why would anyone want to assume such a detached, nerve-rattling, bossy role, especially since goalies are constantly at risk of becoming instant pariahs? It doesn't take much to disappoint. Not diving the right direction. Not grabbing the high, arcing pass before it gets headed. Not throwing your unprotected body across the path of the attacker so that all that precious flesh and bone blocks the shooting angles.

But we have still not mentioned the other main reason for avoiding the goalkeeping position: physical pain! I remember our keeper at Good Shepherd Academy in Ethiopia and how he once dove pell-mell onto a ball just as the opposing striker took a shot. He essentially tackled the ball *and* the foot of the attacker, which meant he took a hard kick to the head. Dazed, he lay on the ground, clutching his skull. But the kicker was writhing too, clinging to his knee, which had doubled in size, dislocated. I still cringe, remembering how the opposing coach, a stern Ethiopian man, raced to the boy, lifted his distorted leg, then yanked it to reset it, and how our goalie rolled over in horror as the other boy screamed.

Whatever others may say, soccer is a contact sport, and the contact will be especially jarring in the mouth of the goal. It's unavoidable because every offensive player has been trying throughout the game to get the ball into that upright, rigid rectangle—twenty-four feet wide and eight feet high—and every goalie has been determined throughout the game to keep the ball out of that space.

I am reminded also of Mike, our goalie at Rift Valley Academy in Kenya, and how he would howl in the shower. As our varsity starter, Mike regularly laid himself out sideways, scraping his hips across the rutted ground. Whereas I might bruise a shin or scuff the side of my calf when executing a slide tackle, Mike constantly ripped away the skin on both hips, creating turf burns that scabbed then tore open again. When he stepped into the shower, the water and soap would make those wounds blaze, and he would let out involuntary shrieks.

Back then, in Kenya, no high school goalies had hip pads. I don't think Mike even had gloves, which might have been introduced at a professional level in Europe but were practically unknown in Africa. However, from what I could tell, Mike didn't think in terms of protection. He had a devil-may-care attitude about every aspect of life.

He was a brash guy who loved to blast music down the hall of our boarding school dorm, picking songs that were off-limits for us as missionary kids, such as "Bat Out of Hell" by Meat Loaf. He loved danger. In fact, he would later immigrate to southern Africa to become a safari guide and big-game hunter, which makes all the sense in the world, given his outlook as a youth. When I think of Mike now, I imagine him crawling as close as he can to a lion or rhino before taking aim. I imagine him waiting as the animal charges, because afterward he will feel so alive.

One last thing: goalkeepers have a natural tendency to become a team's lightning rod. The position demands a sturdy ego and a radical belief in one's own abilities. How else will you survive? So it's no surprise, really, that you can get a goalie like Hope Solo from the US Women's National Team, who declared that if she had been allowed to play instead of being benched for the 2007 World Cup game against Brazil, they would have won instead of losing 4–1.

Solo, whose name seems comically apt, refused to accept her coach's decision to start an older goalie with more experience. She stated bluntly, "It was the wrong decision, and I think anybody that knows anything about the game knows that. There's no doubt in my mind I would have made those saves."

Afterward, Solo was shunned by her teammates for not supporting the coach as expected. But when the 2008 and 2012 Olympics came around, she proved just how good she really was, helping to win both.

Or what about the firebrand Argentine goalie Emiliano Martínez, who, after receiving the Golden Glove at the men's 2022 World Cup, held the gilded object at his crotch and made pelvic thrusts, seeming to mock all the other teams and their goalies? I'll be honest; he turned me off at that moment, marring what was otherwise a beautiful celebration for the Argentinian championship team. However, when I look back on his undiplomatic behavior, it strikes me that maybe he simply couldn't help himself—cocky as ever, individualistic, full of the fuck-you attitude that helped him to make instantaneous, game-winning dives over and over during that tournament.

Crazy. Maybe it takes just a bit of that for a goalkeeper to really succeed. And maybe I have always been just a bit too measured to play the position. The few times I have had to play the role, agreeing to take a turn because we had no goalie, I have handled the ball well enough, scooping it up or leaping to catch it. But I have been too hesitant—too chicken, really—to make the necessary sideways dives when a ball was rocketing toward a corner of the net. More importantly, I have hated the feeling that so much was on my shoulders.

I once found myself talking to an eighth grader who played

keeper for a club team in Lawrence, Kansas. He had already played keeper for five or six years, so I asked him why he liked the position. "I mean, I would hate it," I admitted, "because at any moment, I might disappoint everybody."

He just grinned. "Yeah, but what if you make a stop? What if no one else can make the stop, but you do it all by yourself? There's nothing like that. It's like I've got my own special powers."

What could I say but yes?

A toast to him and all the other goalies. The most unique players on the field—and the toughest!

DID YOU KNOW?
Why All the Goal-Scoring Hullabaloo?

First-time viewers of soccer games are sometimes bored, finding the zeal of soccer fans baffling. How does one appreciate an hour and a half of random kicking and chasing with only the occasional goal, or two—or none? What's compelling about all the aimless running and kicking, the backpedaling of players who flick the ball in the wrong direction? Why such bother over keeping control if the stupid ball is nowhere near its presumed target?

Credulous, uninitiated viewers also wonder why goal scorers race to the corner of the field. Why do they push away chasing teammates, sliding on their knees or ripping off their shirts?

Well, here's the main reason: that longed-for moment has been delayed thirty minutes, fifty minutes, sometimes even ninety minutes. That singular instant of success has been on hold for what has felt—in the realm of athletics—like "eons."

Basketball players may achieve a goal-scoring success every ten or twenty seconds. American football players may get one every five or ten minutes. But soccer players often wait through a whole game, may have to play an overtime, may even have to go home and come back for a second game to get just one rare lightning strike.

In fact, at any given time, there are professional teams around the world that are struggling to get a goal after multiple games. Currently, Leicester City, in the Premier League, has gone four games without a goal. The Czech team Pardubice and the Egyptian club Ismaily are each on five-game scoreless streaks. An Argentine team, Vélez Sarsfield, has failed to score in seven straight matches. And a team in Azerbaijan, Sumgayit FK, just set the record for the longest goal drought in world soccer history: ten consecutive matches.

So yes, a goal gets a lot of celebration. Sing it out. Hold it as long as you can. *Gooooooooooooooal!*

8

¿Hablas Español? ¿Hablas Fútbol?

For a year, straight out of grad school, I lived in Elgin, Illinois, while working for a foundation that offered training to writers and editors in Africa and Asia. Having moved to the area, I did what I always did—went looking for soccer players. And the group that I found, scrimmaging at the back of a weary park, turned out to be mainly migrant workers from Mexico.

I wandered over in shorts, carrying cleats. "Can I join?" I asked a guy who was playing goalie.

He shrugged and called to a teammate in Spanish. Then that guy glanced back, spun away, and jerked his arm as if pulling a rope.

"Si," said the guy in the goal. "Bienvenidos."

So that's how I became part of a Spanish-speaking soccer team playing in a Latinx league that stretched across Chicago.

"Alejandro," they named me, giving me the ID card of a player who had gone AWOL from the team.

Only a couple of these new teammates spoke more than a few phrases of English, but they grinned when they called to me during warm-ups, "Alejandro, hola. Qué pasa?"

I stumbled over a few memorized greetings and tentative responses, but mainly I listened for clues I could understand. With time I knew that "ándale" meant move it, "centro" meant pass the ball to the middle, and "bueno" meant not bad, guy.

Despite my very limited Spanish, they were wonderfully

welcoming. After games, they would lounge on the grass, drinking beer from an ice chest and eating cold watermelon. "Sientate," they would demand, patting the ground.

I couldn't understand three-quarters of what was said during those laid-back lounging times, but they didn't mind me being a quiet listener—at least most of them didn't. The exception was a dour thirty-year-old who stared at me sometimes as if I were a problem that needed fixing. The others slapped me on the shoulder and said congratulatory things about my playing while he just stared sternly.

This dour guy, I eventually realized, was a regular source of contention, not just for me but for everyone else. He was always the one to make a mean-spirited play midgame, triggering reactive outbursts. He was positioned in the backfield like me, and I would wince when he intentionally hip-checked another player or when he grabbed a jersey after being beaten by a nimble forward. More than once, I saw him snag dribbling opponents at the ankle, tripping them.

It was inevitable that competitors would get mad and erupt. One day, though, this guy's fouls were particularly egregious. He knocked several opponents to the ground instead of trying to steal the ball. And he got away with it because the referee was afraid to card him.

Finally, an attacking striker outplayed him in front of the goal, winding up to shoot, and our guy yanked the player's jersey so hard that he missed the ball and fell over. Then the referee blew his whistle, but whatever he was going to call, it was too late. His words were drowned out by a dozen enraged voices, cursing: "Puto." "Pinche estúpido." "Hijo de puta." Then the entire opposing team raced at the offender, who spun in circles, trying to dodge fists.

The other guys on my team knew that this player had gone too far. Some cursed in frustration. But loyalty trumped disapproval, so most of them sprinted into the melee, punching too. Even a couple from the bench leaped into action, which left me walking over to the two or three conscientious objectors, who shrugged as if to say, "This is definitely not worth it."

I was still sitting there when the mean-spirited teammate who had started the whole thing came racing by. He stooped and clutched a loose soccer shoe. Then he dashed back into the action, swinging cleats at people's heads.

Where was the referee? I wondered, and I scanned the field for a yellow-striped shirt. I shouldn't have been surprised, I suppose, but the ref was already in the parking lot with two linesmen. All of them jumped into cars and sped away.

How that fight stopped, I have no idea. However, after the visiting team realized there would be no more playing, they drifted down the far sideline and headed to their cars. Then our guys plopped down on the warm grass as usual and opened the ice chest. Bottles of Budweiser and Corona came out, and someone with a bottle opener passed it around. Someone else placed a fat watermelon on the substitute bench and cracked it open with a pocketknife.

There were reddish lumps on a few faces, but everyone seemed to be in high spirits as they chomped on the watermelon and tipped the beer bottles back—as if freed now to be completely at ease. One of the oldest players muttered something wry about the fellow who had caused the ruckus, and all the others laughed sardonically, looking over at the offender, who was seated on the perimeter of the group. He just stared at the vacant soccer field with a sour expression.

Another player went into lecture mode, clearly not happy about what had happened. I could tell he was hoping the rest of the guys would jump in to support whatever he was saying. He looked around for confirmation, but everyone was quiet.

Then the troublemaker said something snide, getting a wave

of laughter, and I could tell he had been welcomed back into communion. He grinned devilishly. When his eyes met mine, he winked.

I didn't like what he had done. I knew that he would do it again, causing further trouble. But I also knew that it was not my place to say anything, and I could tell that there was a tacit agreement among the guys. We were all part of the same team, flawed as it might be.

"Alejandro," the guys shouted as I finally lifted myself off the grass, "buen juego."

I smiled, happy to receive a compliment. I slapped a hand or two. Then I started across the field.

"Hasta luego," they shouted. And I echoed it back: "Hasta luego."

Tensions always exist when crossing borders, and that can make one want to stay home. However, for more than fifty years, soccer has served for me as a sort of passport, and I'm thankful for that. Of course, I didn't get to know those teammates deeply during a single season of summer soccer. I was too hampered by my limited Spanish. And playing on a Mexican American team is not the same as traveling to Mexico. However, in my imagined passport, there is an imagined Mexican visa from the 1980s, and I carry it proudly, glad to have seen life—for just a bit—from yet another perspective.

9

One Game but Many Points of View

Although I have lived in the US since my early years in East Africa, and though I have traveled overseas for only short stints as an adult, the international flavor has never gone out of the game for me. In college, I opted to keep soccer as something fun, not dictated by a coach, so I played on intramural teams. The players were a wonderful conglomeration of nationalities, having come to the US from Costa Rica, Saudi Arabia, France, Brazil, Nigeria, Iraq, Egypt, England, Mexico, Malaysia, you name it. And the same was true during graduate school, when I played for the official club team at the University of Kansas.

Decades later, I cherish memories of teammates like tall, lanky Hans from Germany, who ruled the backfield by heading the ball away or booting it to the other end. I remember with fondness Achilles from Argentina, who had more than a touch of the Maradona ability to make magic with his feet. At times, he would make a ball seem to virtually disappear. In fact, Achilles so confounded a less accepting, more monochromatic team of fraternity players that a fistfight broke out, triggered by racial slurs, which only goes to show that when tensions erupt, they are often due to players who have not fully realized or accepted the cross-cultural nature of the game.

After grad school, I began a job in Chicago, where I played with the Mexican guys who nicknamed me "Alejandro." I also played pickup games with a group of Assyrian refugees, who tended to warm up by running sprints with militaristic uniformity. Then I got married, which led to a new home in the suburbs north of Chicago. Nevertheless, once again, a very international group of men welcomed me when I chanced upon them practicing on a baseball field.

We were a strong rec-league team, winning over thirty games in a row. But what stays with me most are the colorful ways those teammates interacted, such as Little Joe, who gesticulated and insisted in patently Italian fashion that we needed to stop relying on his dribbling so much—"Fake the pass. Look to me, but take the shot. Trust me, guys." Or Glynn, our team manager, cautioning me in his crisp British accent, "A sweeper is a defender. Don't stray too far." Or Gus, who had gone to a Greek Orthodox seminary and liked to hang out after games, talking not about soccer but about existential things like the harrowing survival of his ancestors in Turkey during the massacre of Armenians.

Over and over, my horizons were expanded by such friendships. I got to see life through other eyes, which made me curious to see more. And that's still true today. When I finish a pickup game here in Kansas, I will sometimes join a group that grabs drinks at a coffeehouse, everyone wearing wrinkled sweats and soccer sandals. Those gatherings often go beyond any predictable soccer banter. Recently, for example, we fell into conversation about our attitudes toward money.

Song, who had rebelled against his police-chief father and the bureaucratic path his father was mapping out for him, emigrated from Korea to the US even though it meant having to sleep on a park bench for weeks, then having to sleep on the floor of a Chinese restaurant where he found work. He bought a push mower and borrowed a friend's pickup and took to mowing lawns at a huge mall, working from 6 AM to 9 PM to make enough money to continue his studies. He learned a fierce independence in the process, refusing to call and ask his father for financial support.

I, by contrast, lived as a missionary kid with parents who were focused on spiritual matters, and though that meant getting by without many of the comforts that went with American wealth, such as electricity or running water, I learned that such comforts do not equal happiness. I still don't like to shop, since buying stuff means having more stuff to take care of.

As for Oscar, whose parents slipped into the US from El Salvador forty years ago, though he had little money while growing up, he learned that he could still be generous. His parents scraped a meager living as janitors at Kansas State University until they could start their own independent janitorial service. "Like all parents, they made mistakes," he said. "But I've got tremendous respect for the way they gave and gave. There weren't many people from south of the border when they arrived, but more started to come—from Mexico and Honduras and Guatemala—and my parents were always giving, not just money but time and energy. That's what amazes me still. They were always helping people to get clothes or find a used car or get a job."

As Oscar described that aspect of his upbringing, I realized just how much it continues to shape the way he lives. He is forty-eight now, and though he worked in banking for years, he jumped out of that so that he could become an independent executive coach for businesspeople. Money is not the point, he says. He wants to help people live better, pursuing healthy goals in their work and relationships.

It shows on the field too, where Oscar outhustles guys who are twenty years younger, shouting coach-like encouragements. I used to arrive at the field at our usual 9 AM starting time, and he would already be out there with an awkward junior high boy whom he had invited to play. Oscar would empty a net bag of soccer balls and start passing them to the kid, coaching him on how to trap the ball, how to turn, how to pass, how to shoot.

And here's the thing: today, if the same boy shows up for a

game, he's not awkward anymore. He plays with the smart, precise movements and decisions that Oscar encouraged in him. He doesn't hang on to the ball too long or take premature shots. And he is welcomed right along with the rest, having earned the respect of a whole group of college-aged students and older men and women.

Soccer is the point, in a way, but it is also *not* the point, because something more important is being explored out there on the pitch. And I am convinced that the wider the array of backgrounds, the deeper the discoveries can become. In that sense, the hyperenthusiastic fictional soccer player Dani Rojas, who stars in the TV series *Ted Lasso*, is not far off the mark with his goofy motto: "Fútbol is life!" To play is to be put into relationship with a range of interesting people—and to potentially learn how to live better.

DID YOU KNOW?
Just How Universal Is This Game?

The globe-spanning World Cup, played every four years, is a good measure of how widespread soccer has become. Until recently, 32 national teams could qualify, but because the game has increased so much in popularity, 48 teams will be allowed in the 2026 World Cup, and that's still only 48 out of a whopping 208 competing nations.

Europe alone has 55 teams, which are contending for 12 slots in the 2026 World Cup. South America has 10 nations contending for 6 slots. North America, Central America, and the Caribbean have 32 teams, but they are competing for yet another 6 slots. Fifty-four African teams are competing for 9 slots. Forty-six Asian teams are competing for 8 slots. And 11 Oceanian teams are competing for 1 slot. Then a whole set of runners-up will battle it out in a complicated intercontinental playoff that determines the last 2 slots.

Because of how many teams engage in this immense contest, 80 nations have qualified since the World Cup began in 1930. Only 8 have actually won, and only 1 has qualified all 22 times—Brazil—but every time the Cup comes around, there are surprise qualifiers. In 2022, no one expected Wales. In 2018, no one expected Iceland. And who would have expected Israel as one of those dark horses? Or Haiti, or Kuwait, or Trinidad and Tobago? However, every one of those tiny nations has broken into the big time at some point since the first World Cup occurred in Uruguay nearly a hundred years ago.

Who will make it next? That's the question. Maybe Kazakhstan? Grenada? Madagascar? You may smile and shake your head, but anything is possible, which is only more evidence of how universal soccer has become!

10

Offsides! Yankee Fans in a Premier Palace

Getting to attend a Premier League game in London, especially the opening game of the season, is no easy task for a visiting American. And getting three seats together is tougher, especially if you are hoping to sit with Arsenal fans while Arsenal is playing away at Crystal Palace. Somehow my son Luke prevailed, after endless online searches, and I decided to bankroll the ridiculously expensive endeavor, and then my other son, Conrad, decided to join the fun, having supported Arsenal for years.

This all happened in August 2022, as Arsenal was beginning what would become their best season in twenty years, staying on top of the standings until Manchester City painfully plucked away the league title. I was in Canterbury, England, as that season launched, traveling with my wife for our thirty-fifth wedding anniversary, and we had invited our grown sons to join us for a bit, not expecting this extra event. Cathleen decided she was happy to stay in Canterbury till after the game, so I left her to meet Conrad and Luke. Unfortunately, though, they had made an ill-advised side trip and missed a train, which meant they got to the Crystal Palace train station only fifteen minutes before kickoff.

I shook my head in disbelief as they came out of the station dragging full-size wheeled suitcases. There were no lockers there, and all taxis were taken, so what could we do but set off on the mile-long hike to the stadium, grinding down the plastic wheels of those suitcases? As the cases clacked along and the crowd thickened, I kept preparing the two young men for disaster. I was convinced that no stadium was going to let fans enter with luggage. To my amazement, though, at the ticket booth we were told to simply throw our bags next to a dozen others stowed behind the counter. Then they pointed us around the looming structure toward our designated entrance, and we went jogging up a long hill.

As we rounded the far end of the stadium, we could hear an enormous chorus chanting a familiar tune:

> You are my Palace, my only Palace,
> You make me happy when skies are grey,
> You never know just how much I love you,
> Please don't take my Palace away.

The three of us found ourselves laughing at the cheery devotion of the Palace fans. Their excitement, even if it opposed ours, was palpable.

At the security check, we had to wait in a crowded line. We heard a tremendous roar as we pushed through the cage-like turnstiles. Clearly the game had begun, so we dashed to the steps that would take us down into the actual seating area. I was in such a rush that I didn't anticipate our entry into the stadium proper. However, once we came around the last corner, we were met by a glorious sight: a sweeping bank of cheering fans lit up by late-afternoon sunlight and, above them, another sweeping rank of fans, topped by an immense curved awning that extended like the bill of a huge baseball cap.

To enter that stadium was doubly powerful because I was doing it with Conrad and Luke. I could see my own exhilaration mirrored in them. We jogged down the stairs, past security people in neon-yellow vests that said "Steward." We turned away from the end-of-field seats, then wove through the streaming crowd to our place near midfield under a low, flat ceiling raised on iron posts. Everyone was on their feet, shouting. To be precise, all the Crystal Palace fans were shouting, since the only side-by-side seats Luke had been able to find were in the middle of a huge section of home-team fans.

We squeezed down a row of hollering men, and as soon as we had secured our seats, a burst of cursing went off. The replay on a giant screen at the far end showed that Arsenal had been awarded a corner kick, but the Palace fans were convinced the ball had come off an Arsenal player.

"Bloody hell," someone bellowed.

"The ref's a twat," someone added. "Where do they find these morons?"

Further curses broke out as one of the Arsenal forwards got a head on the long, arcing kick and almost knocked it into the goal. I surreptitiously faked clapping, and Conrad reached over to clamp my hands.

When we had told English acquaintances that the only seats we could find were among Palace fans, they had cautioned, "Best be quiet, lads. Quiet as church mice." So we did just that, jammed up there between rows and rows of people in blue-and-red-striped jerseys. However, each time Arsenal completed a particularly good play, Luke would lift his cell phone to show us the Arsenal logo, a red shield with a golden cannon, and we would grin conspiratorially.

I had coached both of these guys when they were in grade school, and I had played pickup soccer with them ever since. I had also watched, with pleasure, as they joined the same fantasy soccer league and discovered a shared loyalty to Arsenal. As a result, just helping to support their chosen team was a delight—maybe even more so because the three of us were seated in a sea of "enemy" fans.

A new chant broke out:

Walking down the Holmesdale Road
To see the Palace Aces . . . oh the lads.
Should have seen us coming,
Everywhere was red and blue,
Everyone was running,
All the lads and lasses,
All the smiling faces.

Then the crowd roared as a Crystal Palace player stole the ball and fired it down the sideline to a galloping teammate, who almost shook off the last defender.

Instead, though, the tenacious Arsenal fullback tipped the ball away and took possession, moving back toward midfield. A quick pass from him, and an Arsenal attacker broke into the Crystal Palace penalty box to shoot. The ball was deflected out-of-bounds, which meant we were awarded another corner kick, and this time one of our forwards got his head on the crossing ball perfectly, snapping it down under the diving goalie so that it bounced into the net.

What dismay! The Palace crowd went into a mass fit, throwing hands in the air and cursing. At the same time, we began to hear, down at the far end where all the Arsenal fans were sectioned off, a new chant:

Ooh to,
Ooh to be,
Ooh to be a
Gooner

Both of my sons grinned, and I chuckled, realizing that the heavily accented last word was "Gunner"—the term for an Arsenal supporter.

Later I would ask Luke who exactly put that header into the goal. I'm terrible about remembering such details, but he would confidently remind me that it was Martinelli, the Brazilian wonder boy who'd signed with Arsenal as an eighteen-year-old and helped Brazil win gold at the 2020 Olympics. I would also ask who scored the second Arsenal goal, and he would tell me it was Saka, the Londoner whose parents had emigrated from Nigeria. Like Martinelli, Saka had signed with Arsenal at a very early age—only seventeen—and he was only twenty-two when we saw him play, but he had already been named Arsenal's Player of the Season a year before.

None of that really registered for me in the moment, though, because I was more taken by the sheer experience of being up there in the stands with all the shared camaraderie—the proud chanting, the yearning cheers, the despondent groans. And I was struck by how wonderfully British it all was, this game between a team that had originated with munitions workers at the Royal Arsenal in 1886 and a team that had been started in 1861 by a group of amateur players who lived near the immense Victorian glass hall created for the first World's Fair, dubbed the Great Exhibition.

One of the most memorable aspects of the whole experience was not even a part of the game. At halftime, an all-male grounds crew ambled onto the soccer pitch carrying pronged pitchforks and began poking at the short, immaculate grass. Sprinklers came on, and the lawn guys walked leisurely in the gaps between oscillating sprays, doing their meditative aerating. Giving such attention to the turf seemed classically British—like an extension of the gardening skills so evident in the front gardens of virtually every English house, where tiny alpine flowers cascade down stone walls, bold blooms tremble in window boxes, and carefully shaped shrubs mark perimeters.

My sons remember clearly how Arsenal's two goals unfolded. With regard to the second one, they recall how Saka fired a bullet-like shot across the field from far right that went into the goal after deflecting off the foot of a particular Palace defender, Guéhi, who was born in Côte d'Ivoire and raised in London, where his parents had emigrated when he was an infant. They would remind me of such details later. But what stays with me now, as I look back, is those contemplative groundskeepers who strolled the football pitch so meditatively, poking at indiscernible divots. I remember too the grins of the guys as we took a selfie in the middle of the raucous crowd. Then the long barrier of seats that were covered with yellow vinyl from the top of the stadium to the bottom to separate the home crowd from the visiting crowd.

Lines of stewards were stretched out on each side of that barrier as we exited. They were wearing neon-yellow and -orange vests labeled "Arsenal Response Team" or "Deputy Safety Officer," and they simply stood in the way of anyone who might consider crossing the covered seats. No one made a run for it. However, people shouted taunts. They yelled and laughed and cursed. And when we stepped out onto the street at last, where the sun had gone down without our realizing, the last thing that stands out to me is a big cluster of joyful Arsenal devotees hopping up and down in the middle of the street, arms over each other's shoulders, chanting,

We won the league Anfield.
We won it at the lane,
Stamford Bridge, Old Trafford.
No one can say the same.
Mikel Arteta's army,

We're Arsenal through and through.
We'll sing it in the North Bank,
And in the Clock End too.
Allez, Allez, Allez,
Allez, Allez, Allez.

Caught up in the celebration and united with Arsenal fans at last, we rocked our shoulders in time with the chant. We lifted our arms. We did a little jig in the middle of the blocked-off road as Crystal Palace fans streamed past. And that moment of revelry is something the three of us can return to and cherish in the years to come—a shared moment that bonded us in a new and delightful way.

11
Pride vs. Spirit

A couple years later, our son Luke was the one who made us aware that the championship of the National Women's Soccer League was taking place in Kansas City and on an evening when he would visit. He called from Des Moines to point out that the game would occur the same weekend he planned to drive down and only an hour from our house in Topeka.

Cathleen and I took the hint. A quick scan of tickets showed there were only expensive seats remaining, some priced as high as $995. We wanted to oblige. However, our house had just been broken into and our car stolen, forcing us to shell out for new locks, a rental, and then bodywork to repair the recovered but damaged vehicle. The cheapest side-by-side tickets we could find were $150, which was actually $175 once you paid the added fees. Since three would cost $525, Luke kindly deferred, noting that our own team—the Kansas City Current—had lost in the semifinals, so even though the championship would be in their stadium, we wouldn't get to see them.

We released the whole idea and agreed to go listen to jazz instead. However, on a whim, Luke took one last glance at ticket prices and reported that StubHub was now unloading tickets for only $50.

"Dad, Marta is going to play, and probably for the last time," he said, knowing I am a sucker for great players from other nations, especially older ones. "And Trinity Rodman is on the opposing team," he added, knowing I had tracked Rodman's infamous basketball-playing father when I'd lived in Chicago, where he had helped to win the NBA championship alongside Michael Jordan.

So that was how Cathleen and I ended up downtown in Kansas City with Luke on a chilly November evening, parking our remaining undamaged car at an abandoned strip of unlit gravel, then walking half a mile across dark railroad tracks to reach a set of jammed lots next to the Current's new stadium. We wove through a column of crawling vehicles along with a throng of exuberant fans, whose breath sent little puff-clouds into the night air, and I got a kick out of all the team gear—purple-and-blue jerseys for the Orlando Pride and bright yellow for Washington Spirit. Women and daughters were the majority, but I saw numerous fathers and young men, and almost everyone was proudly displaying anything remotely soccerish, including rainbow-striped scarves and knit hats with team logos.

This is where I must confess, being as old as I am, that what I was seeing as we approached that stadium was somewhat mind-boggling. When I was a teenager in the seventies, living only one hour north of Kansas City, a crowd like this was unthinkable. Back then, soccer was treated like something weirdly un-American. According to the guys on my high school football team, the sport was a Honda—not worth comparing to a Ford or Chevrolet. There were absolutely no boys' soccer teams within a sixty-mile radius. And girls' teams? Even more outlandish! Girls might run track, but the guys I knew treated them like they should leave team sports alone, sticking to the sidelines as cheerleaders. How amazing, then, to see so many fans going to an actual professional women's game.

A lot of the girls were wearing face paint and Spirit or Pride gear. And among those who weren't, many were wearing loyal KC Current gear, such as the teen behind us, who was in a bright red jacket with a signature stripe of teal down each side. Seeing her jacket, I couldn't resist asking her and her parents whom they would be rooting for.

"The Washington Spirit," they blurted, as if the question had an obvious answer.

"Why the Spirit?"

"Because Tracy here just spent a week training with their goalie."

"Aha," I replied, "so you are one of those crazy girls who doesn't mind diving in front of bullets!"

She laughed and nodded enthusiastically.

"And where did this goalie training happen?"

I expected to hear North Carolina or California or maybe Florida due to the warm weather, but instead she said simply, "Blue Valley."

"You mean the Blue Valley right here near Kansas City?"

"Yup!"

Incredible. A professional goalie training high school girls here in our Midwestern state, and in the final weeks of her season.

"Impressive!" I said, giving her a thumbs-up. But since we had reached the entrance and a security guard was emptying everything out of my wife's backpack, we had to wave goodbye.

Eventually, we slipped back into a striding stream of fans, circling the eastern end of the stadium. Then Cathleen, Luke, and I climbed a couple flights of stairs to find ourselves standing at midfield about twenty rows back, which gave us a lovely view of the entire stadium. I was struck immediately by the compact beauty of this brand-new space. The sleek contemporary design includes a rounded outer wall and a curving canopy. Also, one end of the field opens onto the vista of the converging Missouri and Kansas Rivers, in keeping with the team's name, Current.

Having tracked news about the stadium's construction, I knew something most out-of-staters would not realize: this structure wouldn't exist without the generosity of a rather famous donor couple—Kansas City Chiefs quarterback Patrick Mahomes and his wife, Brittany.

It was Brittany who first saw potential for a professional women's team in Kansas City, having played collegiate soccer plus a year of professional soccer in Iceland. With the help of her superstar husband and an entrepreneurial couple named the Longs, the team was launched in 2020. Now, only four years later, the stadium was completed—the first stadium designed specifically for a professional women's soccer team rather than being borrowed from some men's soccer or football team.

I could see that the size was perfect, accommodating eleven thousand fans rather than the horde of seventy-six thousand who get stacked into the enormous Chiefs stadium where Mahomes plays. Our seats were at midfield, but a quick scan showed that no seat would be a bad one. I was intrigued too by the open end of the stadium to the west. It was dark out there, absolutely pitch-black, and I realized that the unlit darkness must be due to the hidden Missouri River. As we sidled to our seats, a player who was warming up accidentally overshot the goal by ten or fifteen feet, which meant the ball rocketed over a low wall and faded into the blackness beyond. I chuckled, thinking of the sphere splatting down and then floating away, perhaps to drift clear to St. Louis.

I felt delighted by the bright, condensed energy of the Current stadium. Everything was wonderfully close and visible. We had barely sat down, however, when a rowdy row of Washington fans sidestepped to their seats in front of us, and since they wouldn't sit, we had to stand. They threw arms in the air, high-fiving each other. Then they cupped their hands and started to bellow in support of the starting Spirit lineup.

One of the things that struck me as we listened to that lineup being announced was how international the players were. The Washington starters included players from England, Colombia, Canada, and Côte d'Ivoire. As for the Orlando team, not only Marta but two other starters were from Brazil. Then there was a Zambian forward and an English goalie.

I don't know why such internationalness should have surprised me except that I tend to pay special attention to women's soccer during the women's World Cup, which means I generally see the very American lineup that constitutes our national team. Because of that lineup, I think I was assuming the US league would be very American as well.

Not so. Much like the Premier League in England, which is a top destination for international players, the US National Women's Soccer League has become a leading destination. And no wonder our national team competes so well—they are constantly getting to play alongside or against many of the strongest players in the world.

The game began, and we cheered along with both sides, simply enjoying the level of play. It was fiercely physical down there, with players going to the turf as they collided for headers or slid to block a pass. Thirty-eight-year-old Marta made a couple impressive runs for Orlando, dribbling around defenders and firing off a blistering shot from one side of the goal, and it was fun to see her in action, the first player (male or female) to score in five different World Cups and the only player to be voted Best FIFA Women's Player six times. I was hoping for one of her signature roars, the sort that erupts when she has triumphed at the goal. However, quite soon, one of her teammates began to stand out even more for me: the Zambian striker Barbra Banda.

One thing I noticed after a few minutes of watching Banda was that when a ball got passed down the sideline to her, she would inevitably outrun the defender, so I began to concentrate on how she was separating herself. A ball would come spinning down the sideline, and Banda would wait with her back to the defender, which seemed the worst position for winning a sprint. However, as the ball arrived, Banda would suddenly turn into the defender, letting the ball roll past, and then spurt out of that pivot, having put the defender behind her in a delayed start.

Over and over, she used this stunt to her advantage. And oh my, when she got her foot on the ball, it was as if it were magnetically attached. Even though she was at full sprint, the ball stayed so connected to her feet that any defender who was racing alongside could not pry it loose.

After several breakaways like that, Banda's Brazilian teammate Angelina sent a long kick over the defense, and this time, Banda had no head start as she raced the woman marking her. They went sprinting down the side of the field in tandem, and with only a few yards left before the end line, Banda spurted forward as if she would try one last time to get a step ahead and cut toward the goal. Instead, though, she used her outside foot to pull the ball back, coming to a screeching halt and dribbling around the overcommitted defender. One or two quick touches, and she had fired off the sort of shot I can never manage—so low and hard that it skimmed the ground. The Spirit goalie—that same young woman who had come to Kansas City to train the girl from Blue Valley High School—simply couldn't get her hands down quickly enough, so the ball skipped between her foot and the goalpost. Score: 1–nil.

That score came in the thirty-seventh minute, but before the half was over, the Spirit team had nearly equalized, showing that the game could still go either way. And when the second half started, the Spirit almost tied the game again as Trinity Rodman made her first real contribution, getting free long enough to let loose a crossing kick to her Ivorian teammate, Rosemonde Kouassi, who posted up in the goal box, leaping high and redirecting the ball with a snap of her head. The Pride goalie was on it, though—throwing herself to the side and slapping the ball out-of-bounds. And really, that was the last true threat by the Washington team.

Finally, the whistle blew and all the Orlando subs came racing onto the field. Luke smiled, and Cathleen and I smiled back as we watched the celebratory mayhem. Then we slipped away to beat the end-of-game crush. The last I saw was Marta kissing a big shiny cup, but what stayed with me was the astonishing skill of her teammate Banda.

In fact, as soon as we arrived home, I googled Banda to learn more, and I was rewarded with a treasure trove of interesting info. I discovered that she had just transferred to Orlando at the beginning of the 2024 season, receiving the second-highest transfer fee in the history of women's soccer—$740,000. But before coming to the US, she played for a Spanish team and then a Chinese team, winning China's Super League Golden Boot as a mere twenty-year-old when she scored eighteen goals in only thirteen matches. She had also played for Zambia's national team at two Olympics, becoming the leading scorer of any African women's team after twice scoring three goals and doing it in back-to-back games.

Born in Lusaka with five siblings, Banda had learned to play as well as or better than Zambian boys, and that was because she had to play on boy's teams due to how few girls played. She started competing with boys when only seven, and she grew to be unusually tough—so tough that she took up boxing and excelled at that, eventually competing in five professional matches and winning them all.

"Boxing helps keep me on my toes," I read from one of her interviews. "It helps me to think fast and to understand the importance of balancing attack and defense, which is also key in football."

Indeed. That rapid balance of attack and defense—a sudden pivot, a jabbing burst of speed, an unexpected backpedal—those were the kind of bob-and-weave moves you might expect from a skilled boxer. And wow, what a change from the way a woman athlete might have been expected to play a sport, any sport, during my own youth.

Who would have thought, in my 1970s Kansas town, that fifty years later, people would be buying tickets right here to watch women play professional soccer? Or that Kansas City would build the first stadium completely dedicated to a women's team? Or that a player like Barbra Banda would be paid $740,000 to transfer from a Chinese team? Or that in January of 2025, only twenty-five years after the first temporary, struggling attempt at a professional women's league, the Ethiopian American defender Naomi Girma would be paid $1,100,000 to transfer back to the US from England?

Who would have thought? But the future of soccer is here now, and it's as much a woman's future as a man's. The US men had better run hard, or they won't be able to keep up.

DID YOU KNOW?
Pioneers of Women's Soccer

The first recorded soccer match between two fully female teams was in 1881, when a Scottish team defeated an English team 3–0. By 1895, Helen "Graham" Matthews had established a Scottish women's team named Mrs. Graham's XI that played more regularly, despite having their first match stopped after reactive observers stormed the field, outraged by what they considered "scandalous" behavior.

With interest rising among women players, an entrepreneur in London, using the protective pseudonym of Nettie Honeyball, also organized a very popular match that drew ten thousand spectators. North London defeated South 7–1. Unfortunately, though, women's soccer became an even more contentious topic as a result. More of the reactive males called for a halt, and the sport faltered.

It wasn't until World War I, when men were called into military service, that women's soccer surged back into the spotlight. Paradoxically, in the absence of male teams, women organized their own matches, usually to raise funds for injured soldiers. On Boxing Day 1920, a record-breaking match occurred at the Everton Club in Liverpool, drawing fifty-three thousand spectators.

Once again, success brought a backlash. Naysayers were outraged that women players might now be making actual money. They reacted so strongly that the next year, 1921, the Football Association banned all women from using official club facilities, stating that football was "unsuitable for females."

Although it is hard to believe today, that ban lasted half a century. Not until fifty years later, in 1971, was it lifted. As soon as it ended, the first sanctioned English national women's competition began. That Mitre Challenge Trophy Competition culminated at the Crystal Palace Sports Centre, where the Southampton Women's Football Club won against Scotland's Stewarton Thistle.

As for the US, which eventually became the leading nation for women's soccer, no female teams existed until 1950, when four were formed in St. Louis to play in what was called the Craig Club Girls Soccer League. In 1972, due to the new Title IX legislation, gender equality was required in US educational sports, and this provided a big boost, but the first professional women's league in America did not form until 1995, four years after the US won the first FIFA Women's World Cup in Guangdong, China. Michelle Akers scored ten goals at that 1991 World Cup, winning the Golden Shoe and becoming the first US women's soccer icon, soon followed by Mia Hamm, who was named US Soccer Female Athlete of the Year five years in a row. Since 1991, there have been nine Women's World Cups altogether, and the US has won a whopping four!

12
Why I Can't Stop Playing

My wife, bishop of the Episcopal Diocese of Kansas, sometimes has to explain why I am not present for a church-related event. A parishioner might ask in the coffee line after a service, "So where is your other half?" and she'll reply, "He is very religious about his soccer."

That is true in more than one way.

First of all, I am doggedly devout about keeping my soccer-playing schedule. On Wednesday at 3:30 in the afternoon, I drive thirty minutes from our home in Topeka to Lawrence, where I play for two hours with a group of international students and community members at a beautiful turf field between two dorms at the University of Kansas. No stained glass there, but the field boasts a very impressive icon. The center circle is emblazoned with a red-blue-and-yellow Jayhawk.

On Saturday mornings at 8 AM, I head the other direction, driving an hour west to Manhattan to play with a similar group that includes immigrant soldiers from Fort Riley. We scrimmage in an old limestone stadium on the campus of Kansas State University, which features a very different icon: a bronze wildcat, mascot of KSU.

I am very religious about getting to those fields twice a week despite the fact that I am now sixty-four years old. To say that I worship is risking blasphemy, but in the Episcopal tradition, worship includes eucharist, which is Greek for "thanksgiving," and I certainly experience thanksgiving each time I join one of those groups, especially since I come away feeling uplifted in a manner that I need, given my tendency toward chronic depression.

In my case, almost any opportunity to step onto a soccer field with other players has a wonderful spiritual dimension. I know! "Spiritual" is way overused, having been applied to practically every type of situation or activity. My wife, the bishop, would say that spiritual moments are characterized by feeling connected to the Divine, but let me offer a broader definition that works well for me—feeling fully connected to all that surrounds me, which is accompanied by a sensation of being fully alive and fully in the moment.

When I am running after a ball in crisp 45-degree weather or during a classic Kansas heat wave, I am in a heightened physical state of being. If the field is wet and chilly from recent rain or if the artificial turf is burning under the August sun and making my feet broil, then I am very much in my body. I may not be as rationally conscious as I am indoors at my computer, but I am very present, existentially speaking, and that state of being can make me feel spiritually alive, not just physically alive.

I'll take it further. If the opposing team has worked the ball down the field from one player to another until it arrives at someone I need to guard, then I become utterly focused, blocking the lane to the goal and making the opponent second-guess whether to pass or dribble. I am not thinking as much as reacting or following instincts, which means I am not distracted by bills that need to be paid or emails that need to be sent or anything else that goes with my ordinary mental clutter.

This in-the-moment awareness is akin to the state one reaches through meditation, particularly the discipline of mindfulness. By giving close attention to the elemental act of breathing, one can let go of thought. Similarly, through the physical focus of soccer, I find that I am able to let go. I surrender to "being," and I feel a strange release—a kind of blissful internal quiet.

At some point in a game, I might also dash to an open space, setting up a safe line for a teammate's pass, and I might trap the ball, then tap it downfield to another teammate, lifting it just over the outstretched foot of an opponent so that it drops in front of my sprinting comrade. That teamwork will bring me a feeling of being connected as well—another hallmark of spiritual experience.

When moving the ball in unison with others, I become part of something bigger than myself. It's a bit like being in a choir and harmonizing, only the harmonizing is in the form of physical movement. Together, we are a singing dance, all of us choreographed to a larger purpose. And what ecstatic delight if my part of the dance makes it possible for a teammate to snap the ball into the goal! At that moment, I have achieved an assist, which suggests the very thing I am trying to define here. I have gotten along, been connected, not alone or disconnected.

This past winter here in Kansas, a hardy group kept gathering every Wednesday in Lawrence, even if the temperature dropped to 20 degrees Fahrenheit. In Manhattan another group kept playing every Saturday, wearing balaclavas along with gloves, athletic tights, and layered sweats.

Then, one 34-degree Saturday, there was freezing sleet, the one condition that simply makes soccer too miserable to play. Disappointed to have lost my usual workout, I decided to skip church the next morning and make a run to Lawrence so that I could jump into a 10 AM Sunday game. On that particular morning, I was drawn toward the sanctuary of the field rather than an indoor worship space. The only problem was that the sleet had kept on falling through the night, and it was drizzling when I went out to my car around 9 AM.

I stubbornly scraped the iced-over windshield and headed out of town. The air was getting warmer, so fog was settling in. No telling if anyone would show up. Nonetheless, I shot down I-70 and took the exit ramp, then made my way to the field at the KU campus.

I saw no other parked cars, but I swung into a marked slot facing the damp, fog-shrouded field, and I waited. Eventually, one other car pulled up. The driver was Erika, a thirty-five-year-old mother who works as a waitress and plays with tremendous stamina and enthusiasm, often outsprinting male defenders and popping the ball into the net.

The two of us rolled down our car windows and talked through them, looking over the soccer pitch as the fog thinned. She told me how she had first gotten into soccer—by being placed on an all-boys team in fourth grade. And how she had played so well in junior high that her parents had sent her to a special academy for high school. It was a boarding school far away in Florida, where women athletes often got college scholarships and went on to play not only college but also Olympic and professional soccer.

"Hey, do you have a ball?" she asked me suddenly. "Maybe we could just kick it around."

"Great idea," I replied, cheered by the thought of getting onto the field. However, when I looked in my trunk, I was dismayed to find that I had left my practice ball back in the garage.

Still, Erika didn't want to give up, nor did I. So we climbed back into our cars and kept conversing through the open windows, and she told me why she did not get a college scholarship as her parents hoped: "Basically, I developed an eating disorder, and it sapped all my energy. There was no way I could play at my top level."

I was struck by her candor. I felt honored. She had trusted me with something she wouldn't normally tell people. In my case, I don't suffer from an eating disorder, nor have I been physically hampered in my soccer playing other than temporary setbacks from minor injuries. However, as I pointed out earlier, I suffer from clinical depression, and that has been a struggle my whole life, which means I can relate to what she described. In some ways, soccer is actually an antidote for depression, which can become quite isolating when I feel too down to interact.

"That must have been really hard," I replied, "to lose that chance at college ball. I mean, you play so well."

"Thanks. I was angry at first, but now it's okay. Who knows what would have happened? This way, I'm still playing. Not everyone gets to do that, right?"

Twenty minutes had passed. Clearly no one else was coming, so we finally acknowledged defeat, shaking our heads in commiseration.

"Bummer," I said. "I was really looking forward to a game since I didn't get to play yesterday."

"I know," she sighed. "What's up with the rest of the guys? It's really not *that* bad out here. Wet, yeah, but not too cold."

"My thought exactly!"

She smiled. And before rolling up her window, she tossed out one last exuberant declaration: "I just love to play, you know—because it feels so good to be out there."

As she drove away under the rising fog, I thought, *Indeed, indeed*. On those occasions when a group shows up and we take our positions, then start dashing around, I am filled with the opposite of depression. I am filled with life itself.

Hallelujah.

13

Religion vs. Soccer

At my boarding school in 1970s Addis Ababa, a Sunday nap was mandatory—as if lying still were a footnote chiseled across the bottom of the stony commandments Moses carried off Mt. Sinai. Occasionally my parents would arrive from their station in southern Ethiopia to take me and my younger brother away for a weekend at the mission's retreat center, but even then the Sabbath held sway. After sitting through a mandatory worship service next to the dining hall and eating a subdued, soon-we-will-have-to-go-back-to-school lunch, those of us who were teens would beg to do one last thing that was actively fun. Our weary parents, who were quite okay with getting a Sunday nap, would eventually surrender to the pleading, letting us escape down the steep slope to the boathouse—but only *if* we stayed respectfully quiet.

Down we galloped to the shore, where we paddled a canoe onto the rippling crater lake. If we were silent, it was only so that we could glide up to yellow-and-black weaver birds as they constructed their cave-like nests in the shoreline reeds. Inevitably, though, we wanted to do something more interactive, especially if other teens were staying at the retreat center.

Longing for something more playful one noiseless Sunday, we hiked back to the rented cottages and quietly enlisted a pair of friends. Then we sneaked onto the clay tennis court, where we could play a muffled game of two-on-two "socnis" (soccer-tennis).

We served an old, scuffed soccer ball by kicking it over the net. Then we volleyed it back and forth as long as we could, using feet, chest, head, or thighs. We did all this in a top-secret way because we knew that exerting ourselves on the Sabbath was highly questionable. In Old Testament times, someone who broke Sabbath rules could be stoned—an ancient threat that perhaps we could still feel down in our Judeo-Christian bones.

Nonetheless, we couldn't help laughing at the hijinks that went with getting the ball over the net. Then we laughed again, and a door swung open at the nearest cottage, where a seventy-five-year-old British missionary appeared and hissed at us in rage, gray hair aswirl, "Silence!"

This particular missionary was a dentist by the name of Dr. Stamper, and the name suited her well. She could command silence because she had the wrath of God at her back. But it makes me chuckle now to realize that even though we were living in the 1970s, Dr. Stamper was more rigidly conservative than even the famous 1920s Scottish runner Eric Liddell, who became the poster boy for the Sabbath when he was pictured in the film *Chariots of Fire* giving up his chance to race at the Olympics since he would have to compete on Sunday.

I was beginning college when that movie came out, and I felt a strange affinity with the principled Liddell, who would eventually go to China as a missionary and die during the Japanese occupation of World War II. Early in the film, he is pictured coming upon a soccer-playing boy just outside a church service in Scotland, and he gently reprimands him for playing ball on Sunday. However, he also makes an appointment to come back on a different day and jump into the game with the boy's gang of wide-eyed, impressed buddies. His explanation? "I don't want the lad to grow up thinking God's a spoilsport."

Personally, I don't think God is a spoilsport either. Nor does the Anglican bishop of Uruguay, who came to visit Kansas recently and told me that back home in his native Argentina when he was a parish priest, they formed a soccer team from their congregation, meeting weekly to play. The same bishop also pointed out that when Lionel Messi scores, he crosses himself and points to the sky.

Such thankfulness is not merely a Christian concept. Three lesser-known players from a professional team in Indonesia received surprising attention for showing similar gratitude. The trio were playing for Bali United in 2017 when they scored against a rival club. All three paused and took prayer stances, representing their faith traditions. One stood still with his palms meeting in Hindu fashion, another went to his knees and lowered his face to the earth in Muslim prayer, and a third knelt with hands clasped in a Christian manner. A photographer captured this unexpected celebration, and when that photo was posted to the team's Facebook page, it went viral, being shared across Indonesia, where hard-line Muslims had been using the nation's Islamic laws to accuse Christians and Hindus of blasphemy, even causing a former governor to be imprisoned.

A year passed after that unusual incident, and in 2018 the spotlight swung again toward some Asian soccer players with an interesting religious backstory, only this time the entire world was paying attention. Why? Because the players were youths trapped in a flooded cave. A team of Thai teenagers known as the Wild Boars had made the mistake of exploring this cave after a game, going along with their coach, who did not know their escape would be cut off by a flash flood. Three weeks passed before a diver could reach the group, and though they were exhausted and nearly starved, the diver was amazed at how calm they seemed. It turned out that the same coach who had made the mistake of leading them into the cave had trained as a Buddhist monk. Amazingly, he had taught the boys to meditate, which was helping them fight off panic.

This coach's Buddhist example must have had a major impact, because after the Wild Boars were brought out of the inundated cave—donning scuba masks with oxygen tanks and trusting the rescuing divers to swim them through hundreds of yards of black, narrow, flooded tunnels—eleven of the twelve decided collectively to become Buddhist monks. As for the twelfth teammate, Adul Sam-on, he was a Christian, but he had a powerful experience to share as well. Having fled Myanmar as a refugee, he could speak not only Thai and Burmese but also English, which meant he played a crucial translation role for the rescuing British divers. Later he explained that while his teammates had practiced Buddhist meditation, he had practiced his own Christian version. He had relied primarily on the Lord's Prayer and one of his favorite songs, "How Great Is Our God," repeating them over and over. And there in the dark, he received an unexpected revelation: "I couldn't see much in the cave, and I realized that's quite similar to how I can't see God in real life. But I have to trust that He's going to show His power and goodness at the end."

Soon after Adul was brought out of the cave, the world at large learned about his plight as a boy whose parents had spirited him out of Myanmar in hopes of a safer, fuller life. Across the globe in New York, the head of a boarding school arranged for a host family and a full scholarship, inviting Adul to come study. That's just what he did, becoming captain of their soccer team in the process. Today he is a student at Middlebury College, considering a major in medicine but also playing pickup soccer regularly.

I don't know about the strict rules of religion. Part of me is still pushing back against the Sabbath silence that was imposed on me when I was a student at my own boarding school. But I do appreciate the principled discipline that develops in players who have a religious perspective. Jürgen Klopp, the coach of Muslim superstars Mohamed Salah and Sadio Mané at Liverpool United, feels similar respect, having seen the results. Sadio—who was forbidden to play as a child by his father, an imam in Senegal—remains so devoted to the people of his home village that he has helped to build them a hospital, a mosque, and a new secondary school. In 2023, he received the inaugural Socrates Award, which honors a soccer player who has made the biggest humanitarian impact, and this was his response: “Why would I want ten Ferraris, twenty diamond watches, or two planes? . . . I prefer that my people receive a little of what life has given me.”

When Klopp was asked why he, as a coach, allows Sadio and Salah to fast during Ramadan even though it might diminish their ability in key games, his answer was astute: “In this life, there are many things more important than football.”

In some paradoxical way, if players realize that reality, maybe they lift the game for everyone else, making it more than just as an exercise in ego gratification, instead something quite freeing and profound.

DID YOU KNOW? Even Bob Marley Played!

In 1980, an Italian journalist who wrote for music magazines got an interview with the famous reggae musician Bob Marley, who had survived a shooting while preparing for his Smile Jamaica Concert. Marley's new album, *Survival*, had just come out with a pan-African focus that included a song celebrating the anticolonial movement in Rhodesia, which was about to triumph and give birth to the independent nation of Zimbabwe. Marley was willing to meet this young reporter, Mario Calvo-Platero, but he immediately chastised him: "You Italians are terrible people. You attacked the Negus. You killed to conquer."

Marley was a Rastafarian who believed in the divine nature of Emperor Haile Selassie, known as the Negus, who had been forced into exile at the outset of World War II when Italy had occupied Ethiopia. The Italians had dropped mustard gas on villages as they marched toward the capital of Addis Ababa. They had even bombed Red Cross hospitals and ambulances. So what could Calvo-Platero say in response? The only thing that occurred to him was that he had actually been born in Africa—in the nation of Libya—but that news made Marley even more angry: "Another Italian African conquest! Are you the son of colonists? Are you a fascist?"

What finally turned the conversation was that Calvo-Platero explained that he was Jewish. Then Marley relented: "The Jews are survivors. The Negus had a good relationship with them. He descended directly from King Solomon."

They talked a while longer about Emperor Selassie. Then Marley suddenly asked, "Do you play soccer?"

"Of course; all Italians play soccer."

So that is how Calvo-Platero got to do what few visiting foreigners ever did while visiting Kingston, Jamaica, in the seventies and eighties—play soccer in a walled courtyard with Bob Marley and a number of other Rasta musicians. They played on asphalt, with most of the men going shirtless. Calvo-Platero, who had to join the opposing team, found that Marley was tough, playing hard but never fouling. Later, he couldn't recall who had won, but he prizes the backhanded compliment he received from the legendary musician as he finally prepared to jump into a taxi and leave: "You play well for an Italian."

14
Coaching Chaos

When my two sons reached soccer-playing age, I naturally found myself pulled into their orbit as a coach. For the next six years, I coached children's teams, starting with preschoolers and taking them through fifth grade.

The five- and six-year-olds, of course, were a hoot to watch, all mixed together as boys and girls. During games, they tended to move around the field in a swarming clump, as if the ball were a queen bee and they were the hive. If the ball got kicked loose, they scattered and came dashing after it. Then they swarmed into a new cluster unless some child was quick enough to kick the ball away, outsprinting the crowd.

Occasionally, by a miracle, one of those runaway players might actually get near a goal. Then the poor goalie, chained back there between the goalposts like a forgotten prisoner, would hear all the commotion and come out of his or her bored stupor, perhaps dropping a dandelion or ladybug, and the elemental drama would unfold—an actual shot.

Of course, at this age, any attempted "shot" was iffy. Typically, the kid who had outsprinted the crowd would, in his or her excitement, dribble the ball a bit too far away so that it practically rolled up to the goalie like a soft pass. Or if the dribbler was not running down the center of the field, he or she might lose the ball to either side of the goal, sending it over the end line.

There was a lot of amusement with such breakaway "shots." However, one of the most comical was when our least-skilled player—a five-year-old who often seemed deaf to my coaching instructions—kicked the ball loose and took off in the wrong *direction*, toward our *own* goal!

Realizing what was happening, I ran down the sideline next to him, yelling, "Denny, the other way."

His teammates shouted too. And the one law-abiding girl defender who had obeyed my instruction to stay near the goal stood stock-still, not equipped to deal with this paradigm shift.

Nonetheless, sturdy little Denny was so pleased to have the ball and to be outrunning the crowd that he actually began laughing as he neared our horrified goalie. Finally, finally, he was going to have his moment in the sun.

He was wearing oversized hand-me-down cleats, which gave his feet a clownish floppiness. He was a bit overweight and had a classic Midwestern buzz cut. There was a cheerful unselfconsciousness as he wound up and gave the ball one final colossal kick. It bounced off his foot and skipped toward the corner of the goal. It was a true shot for once. Not very hard, but on target.

He had taken this shot from just far enough away that our startled goalie had time to react. As he dashed toward the threatened corner of the goal, part of me wanted the ball to go in. But the goalie, to his credit, dove, and his outstretched hands just barely knocked the ball to the outside of the corner post.

There was a huge cheer from the watching parents—at least those with kids on our team. There was a collective sigh as well.

Would Denny be disappointed? I wondered.

However, true to form, he kept running right past that goal, chasing the loose ball and laughing—happy, happy, happy that, for a few wild seconds, it was his.

15
Wonder Girl

I kept coaching YMCA soccer until my youngest son reached the age of seven. Then a friend and I decided to put together a true club team, including my son and his. At the time, we lived in Newton, Iowa, a community of twelve thousand east of Des Moines, and my buddy and I ended up recruiting kids from three or four local grade schools. They were all boys except two, and of those two girls, one was remarkably talented.

We coached very democratically at this early age, making sure that all kids got onto the field during games, even trying to keep the amount of time equal. In the case of Sophie, who was not so talented, we had to think pretty carefully about where to place her. We occasionally put her right up front, in a highly desired position, because any mistakes she might make were not going to have large repercussions, as they did when a defender failed to slow an attacking striker.

Nikayla, on the other hand, could be trusted to play anywhere. She showed an immediate grasp of the game, instinctively recognizing how all the positions fit into a larger system. She made instant, exact passes. She ran everywhere with amazing perseverance, including coming back to defend the goal. We could see immediately that she was a born midfielder, and she started in that position all three seasons that we coached the group.

How fun to put a player where he, or she, naturally excels. Over and over, Nikayla would make surprising interceptions.

Over and over, she would take a few smart dribbles—just enough to find an open lane. Then she would snap a pass to one of our forwards, who would fire on goal. And if our defenders were threatened, Nikayla would come sprinting back, blocking passing lanes and intercepting passes.

Other kids scored a lot, especially the son of my fellow coach, who was already showing the inherent athleticism that would lead him not just to become a standout on the Newton high school soccer team but eventually to break the record for receiving yards on his football team, going on to become a successful wide receiver for the University of Iowa and even playing a year for the Buffalo Bills. Nick had feet too big for his body, but he had a kind of heat-seeking drive that simply could not be denied. As a result, he was a scoring machine. My own son, Luke, was a trusty forward too, racking up almost as many goals. Together, the two were a great offensive combo, especially with Nikayla feeding them the ball. But what I always admired about Nikayla herself was how well-rounded she was as a player.

Nick and Luke weren't going to steal the ball much. They rarely came back beyond midfield. In fact, if we put them on defense, they would instinctively drift forward, unable to resist the gravitational pull of the opponent's goal. Nikayla, on the other hand, was more concerned with where she was needed than whether she scored. She constantly tracked the flow of the game and anticipated where to move. She was a delight to watch, ponytail swinging, face flushed, but clearly thinking as she ran, or perhaps *not* thinking, instead simply seeing the situations and responding.

There was only one flaw in Nikayla's game, as far as I could tell, and that was her reluctance to shoot. It was as if she had been handed a supporting script—not a lead—and she could not imagine any other role. You could count on her to make a last perfect pass but never to receive it and score.

Here's the thing: goals don't happen without assists except on rare occasions. Nevertheless, the glory almost always goes to the scoring player, which is a bit of a shame, since the midfielder is often the one who did the real work. The midfielder makes a steal, takes a few key dribbles, and delivers a long cross or short, snappy pass. However, as soon as the ball finds the net, the striker is the one who races to the corner of the field for a celebratory dogpile. And that is why I found myself really wanting Nikayla to get a taste of the actual scoring experience.

In truth, I wanted some of that experience for the other kids who played defense too. As a result, if we had built a solid lead, I started to intentionally switch players out of their usual positions, letting midfielders and defenders take turns up front. With each successive "first goal," there was a wonderful celebration, not just for the reassigned player but for the whole team, not to mention the proudly cheering parents. Strangely, though, the one I most wanted to score never seemed to get there.

I may be a bit off, but I'm pretty sure Nikayla was the last to rack up a goal, and I clearly recall asking the other kids, at a lopsided game during our second season, to make a point of setting her up. "Nikayla," I said, "remember now that you're our striker, so stay up there. You don't have to come back. And when you get a pass, take a shot. Let it rip, okay?"

Still, she was so inclined to assist that she simply couldn't let herself fire the ball. When another player got a pass to her right in front of the goal, she automatically looked for a teammate and dished it off. It was almost as if the goal was invisible until she had given up the ball.

I still wonder today: had Nikayla's genes been so programmed that they blocked any conscious attempt to take a lead role, or had she been nurtured into her deferential attitude, trained by family members? For that matter, was her deference the result of a wider societal expectation placed on girls?

I will never know. But sometimes when I am on a field with two or three of the intrepid women who join pickup games at Kansas State University or the University of Kansas, I think of Nikayla again, wondering what became of her.

There's a very skilled college student named Anna who joins our games if she is not midway through another season on the official women's team at nearby Baker University. Anna shows no hesitation in coming onto the field with all the male players, a community of talented guys from Syria, Russia, Spain, Nigeria, and so forth. Her father—who plays with us too—is from Thailand, and, as might be expected, Anna looks quite different from Nikayla. However, like Nikayla, she is clearly a trusted participant. The only real difference between the two is that, unlike Nikayla, Anna naturally gravitates to the forward position, outjuking players and shooting on goal. She will often lurk up there, moving into position for a possible shot. That is her chosen domain. And when she scores, cheerful shouts go up from her teammates, accompanied by groans from the other team.

Sometimes, when watching Anna play, I think of grown Nikayla, who must be twenty-seven or twenty-eight years old now. Did she ever break the barrier that kept her from making the final attack on goal? Did she learn that she too had a right to that shooting role?

I hope so. I really do. Because even though she was a natural-born midfielder with oodles of talent, that added option, used every once in a while, would make an important difference. When attacking an opposing goal, the possibility that she might hold on to the ball would keep defenders guessing. Cover the pass or cover the shot? Which one? And with that added weapon, she would be absolutely complete as a midfield wonder.

DID YOU KNOW?
How Referees Took Charge

In the 1840s, as English clubs adopted the emerging rules of modern soccer, they instituted a referee, but his only task, at first, was to keep track of time. English players were expected to act as gentlemen back then, neither cheating nor fouling, and each team had an elected "umpire" to arbitrate if a dispute *should* arise. The problem is that players and fans became suspicious of those elected representatives, fearing bias, so they began to turn to the timekeeping referee for impartiality.

With recurrent altercations, the referee's role became more central. He was seen as an objective third party, so the team-appointed umpires were demoted to the side of the field, becoming line judges by the 1890s. Each would take one sideline and stay on one-half of the field to keep track of offsides or out-of-bounds. Referees, meanwhile, were given expanded authority. One sports analyst estimates that today, contemporary refs make as many as 245 decisions per game, all of which can affect the outcome.

Current technology allows for more certainty than in the past, and refereeing is increasingly supplemented by devices that confirm whether the ball has crossed the goal line, whether a player was truly offsides, etc. At the top level, a new position has been added to the refereeing team, titled video assistant referee

(VAR). Still, the main referee is the one in command out there on the pitch, and never is the referee's authority more evident than when a yellow or red card is pulled out of a breast pocket. As a result, it may be a surprise that those iconic cards did not exist until after 1966. They were "invented" as a result of a controversial quarterfinal at the 1966 World Cup in England. Disturbed by the way that game had turned ugly, a prominent British referee, Ken Aston, was driving home in London and saw a stoplight change. Suddenly he thought, "Yellow, take it easy; red, stop, you're off." So the cards were introduced, becoming a fixture by the next World Cup.

16

No Ball? No Problem!

When I was fifty, I had an opportunity to visit the vast and jumbled township of Soweto on the edge of Johannesburg, South Africa. I was there with a team introducing water-purifying kits to villagers in remote areas, but on arrival, I took a tour of Soweto with a guide who showed us a square mile of small shanties, some made of adobe and tin, others made of concrete blocks, and only a few with anything approaching a yard. We went mainly to view the homes of two Nobel Peace Prize winners: Nelson Mandela and Archbishop Desmond Tutu. The two had lived within a couple hundred yards of each other—inside the restricted perimeter of that ghetto, where they were forcibly separated from whites by the tyranny of apartheid.

Poverty was still apparent everywhere—in the unpainted walls, the dirt paths, and the upright, coffin-shaped outhouses. As part of the visit, the guide asked a local woman if we could see how she made her living, and she invited us into her two-room house, where she had a couple of white plastic five-gallon buckets on the floor next to a handmade wooden counter. The buckets were brimming with brown-flecked froth, and she explained that this was due to fermentation. She made her little bit of income by brewing beer and turning her living room into an evening bar—a "shebeen," as they called it.

When I stepped out of that shanty and waited for the rest of the group, two children came down a dirt path kicking an orange, passing it back and forth with bare feet. The orange got away and rolled close, so I tapped it back, giving them a grin. The older boy was clearly mischievous. He liked this playful response, so he volleyed the orange back, which led to a few minutes of shared passing and juggling.

The path where we were playing was narrow and pocked with craters. A chicken scooted by, staying close to a fence of tied poles that supported a straggly vine. In other words, it was not an ideal soccer pitch. But we improvised within those constraints, batting that orange back and forth and sometimes lifting it off the ground. Since the boys were barefoot, they could get their toes under it, balancing it on a raised foot and gently juggling it. Being shoed, I could only roll it back to them, although I trapped it between my shoes one time, just for fun, then jumped, bringing the clasped orange up toward my butt before twisting and releasing it to one side so that it arced by my hip and over to the waiting boys.

The mischievous one caught it on his thigh and laughed, amused by a fifty-year-old who would even try such a maneuver.

The orange would not last, of course, with all this wear. I could tell it was breaking loose inside the peel. And now it occurred to me that these boys had made a choice—to practice soccer rather than to eat.

I imagine they could still have eaten that orange. If nothing else, they could have sucked the burst cells out of the punctured skin. But they kept playing even though any mistake—a misstep or a single hard kick—and that orange would split, leaking away.

With this realization came a second one: there is a reason that children all over Africa have such amazing dribbling skills. Since the orange was fragile and the boys might still hope to save it, their kicking had to be light and accurate. The same is true for kids from many parts of Africa, who grow up playing with whatever is at hand and doing it *wherever*, not having the resources for regulation-size balls or well-groomed fields. Under those circumstances, they develop very nuanced, exact foot skills.

When I was growing up in Ethiopia, Kenya, and Sudan, I regularly saw kids playing soccer with homemade balls of bundled plastic wound into a sphere by twine. Such balls were the size of a grapefruit, which meant that kicking had to be quite precise. The ball had to be received and dribbled with quicker, defter moves. Also, if the ground was pocked or lumpy, one had to adjust to obstacles instantly.

Here in America, many children receive a regulation ball early in life, but in parts of Africa, playing with a true soccer ball is a privilege. In such settings, a formal game of soccer might not be as much about scoring as keeping possession. How long can you keep the ball away from your opponents, outfoxing them? The longer you do, the more practice you will get and the more esteem you will earn.

Such foot-playing dexterity has given rise to many a standout player across the African continent, such as the Ghanaian star of the 1990s, Abedi Ayew, who grew up in a village on the outskirts of Accra, playing soccer with eighteen siblings. He showed such dribbling finesse in primary school that he was nicknamed Abedi Pele, in reference to the Brazilian great. And he went on to be honored as the African Football Player of the Year three times, playing on the Marseille team in France that won the 1993 UEFA Champions League.

I haven't been to the favelas of Brazil, but I'll bet the same remarkable ball skills—a basis for what commentators call "the beautiful game"—started in much the same way for many Brazilian players long before they became internationally known. I bet it began with a makeshift ball on a pocked dirt patch between a couple of small, simple houses. In fact, the original Pele, whose name was borrowed as a nickname for Abedi Ayew, first learned to dribble with a grapefruit and with a sock stuffed with paper.

He was the greatest soccer player to live, according to many, but he started in this most basic way.

Strategic passing and teamwork can be coached into a player, but basic foot-eye coordination starts earlier, without coaching. If it develops early enough, it is intuitive and instantaneous, which is why I'd like to think that those two boys from Soweto, now in their mid-twenties, are still playing soccer somewhere, hopefully in a freer, bigger, more rewarding setting. I'd like to think that they are earning accolades because of the foot skills they were already developing almost fifteen years ago with a dusty orange on an uneven path shared by a chicken, a straggly vine, and an aging, oddly interactive American.

17

Out in the Open

Over the last forty or fifty years, playing soccer indoors has become more of an accepted option. I was certainly thankful for that option when winter descended in Iowa, where we lived for twenty years. And after moving to a town near the Minnesota border, I was especially thankful.

I played once a week on a wooden floor in a church gym with taped goals marked on cinder-block walls. Up there, near Clear Lake, Iowa, snow could start falling at Thanksgiving and stay until Easter, so I often drove to the church with several feet of new powder plowed onto the shoulders of the road, wondering if other guys would shovel their drives and come. I was relieved to find a few cars parked to the side of the church and to pad around the back of the building, stepping into the foot holes created by whoever had arrived first, then to pull back the metal door and hear the squeaking of tennis shoes and the thud of balls against the walls—the muffled thud of those yellow felt-covered balls that were developed for hard gym floors, since they slide instead of sticking.

With temperatures that often sank to zero degrees Fahrenheit, it was such a gift to find a large, warm, indoor space where I could run and kick, sharing the experience with an eager group of players. We had wacky fun passing balls off the wall and watching them ricochet through clustered players, pinball style, often arriving at the goal from unexpected angles. At one end of the court, there was a cement balcony that created a heavy brow. A smart player could even kick the ball up into that overhang and cause it to bounce down into the goal, leading to lots of laughter.

I'm glad for fond memories like that. But this is all a preface for what I really want to say: I will always prefer outdoor soccer to indoor, and I suspect that is the way most players feel!

I'm convinced indoor soccer will never be as popular because there is something wonderfully elemental and satisfying about playing in the open. On those occasions when I step onto a full-sized outdoor pitch, and when a teammate rolls a ball into the wide-open space so that I can take a practice shot, it is liberating just to move around in so much uncontained, unblocked air. I feel a kind of bodily transcendence. It's the closest I get to levitation.

Of course, in the 1970s in Africa, where I first became serious about the sport, there was no such thing as artificial turf. All our soccer matches were played on soil, either with a mat of rough grass or worn bald. There might be trees or shrubs down the sidelines. There might be African kites flying overhead, spiraling on updrafts. Sometimes smoke from a nearby cooking fire came drifting past, smelling of burned eucalyptus. And to play, as a result, was to be right in nature.

The most dramatic natural setting of all those early soccer experiences was the field at the boarding school in Kenya where I played as a junior and senior. There, we lived in dorms on the steep escarpment that dropped into the Rift Valley, an immense valley that extends all the way from Ethiopia to Malawi. We were several thousand feet above that huge expanse, with miles and miles of dry yellow savannah grass stretched out below us, and because we were so much higher, we lived in a different climate and ecosystem, surrounded by thick forests and wearing jackets against the damp chill at night.

Down on the savannah, giraffes and zebras still wandered, cautiously approaching water holes where lions might be lurking.

And when we looked west along the valley, we could see the hazy silhouette of Mt. Longonot with its crater rim—a whole mountain that rose from the valley floor but seemed a step down from us when we stood on our soccer pitch.

The playing field at Rift Valley Academy offered an excellent view of all that landscape, especially for fans sitting on the ridge created when the field was carved out of the hillside. On that ridge, there were no seats. The slope served as its own natural bleacher. People just plunked down on the grass and cheered, gazing out over all the running players to forty or fifty miles of sprawling savannah.

Every morning during the rainy season, clouds rose from the immense valley below, lifting slowly up the wooded escarpment, which meant that during my senior year, when I came out of the boys' dorm and headed to the cafeteria, I walked in fog. If someone approached from the other direction, they appeared slowly, like a shadow that took on definition.

At that time of year, everything was wet too, including the soccer pitch, with thin puddles scattered here and there. The rain nourished the grass, giving us one of the most enviable fields in Kenya, and we often practiced despite rain, so I got used to the soaked ball turning heavy and my cleats becoming cold and sodden. In fact, one of my most memorable moments at Rift Valley Academy was after a very heavy overnight downpour. We were scrimmaging, and I was positioned at fullback, as usual. One of the guys on the other team made a long, arcing pass toward our goal, sending it over the head of his sprinting forward. I was off to the side, but it was clearly a footrace between me and that player, so I galloped toward where the ball was rolling. As I kicked into my highest gear, I could see that the two of us would arrive at the same moment, meaning my chance of stealing the ball was fifty-fifty. That is, unless I went into a slide tackle.

The field was so wet that every step was splashy, giving off its own wet smack, so I knew that the ground was unusually soft. Without much thought, I threw myself into a slide, gliding along on the puddled surface for a full five yards, and I arrived even sooner than I expected. Not only did I sweep the ball away with my extended leg, rolling it along with the bent one, but the galloping striker had no choice but to leap over me, leaving me completely free. Instinctively, I planted the extended foot and pushed off with a hand, rising right back into a run with the ball neatly at my feet. Then I made a long pass down the sideline to our own forward, which started an unexpected counterattack and led to a goal.

The resulting goal is not what stays with me, however. No, it is the harmony I felt with all the elements around me. I still recall vividly the outdoor physicality of that puddled field and my streaming shorts. The slip-'n'-slide gliding of my legs. The graceful return to my feet. Then the ball coming off my wet shoe hard and straight. I recall the grass stuck to my legs. Even the hovering gray of the clouds farther up the escarpment and the veil of rain down by Mt. Longonot, giving depth to the hidden distances.

Awareness itself—that is what stays with me. And I don't think I ever would have been so aware in a crowded indoor gym with all the attendant sounds echoing off the walls—the squeaking and thunking and grunting and calling out.

What stays with me at the most basic level is the loudness of my own slapping feet and my own gasping breath, the consciousness of existing right there in the middle of everything. Alive!

DID YOU KNOW?
How Indoor Soccer Began

In 1930, when the Uruguayan team had just won the first World Cup and was savoring gold medals from the 1928 Olympics, a teacher from the capital city of Montevideo created an indoor version of soccer to be used at YMCAs. This new version was designed for basketball courts. As a result, it was limited to five players (including a goalie), and games were played for the same duration as basketball—forty minutes. As for goals, they were patterned after goals in another indoor sport: team handball (and therefore were only two meters high and three meters wide).

This new form of soccer spread quickly throughout the YMCA network of South America, and a Brazilian adapted it for use in physical education classes. Soon a confederation had formed, consisting of Uruguay, Brazil, Paraguay, Peru, and Argentina.

Unlike US indoor soccer with its indoor turf, the floor is hard in South American indoor soccer, and there are no hockey-like walls to kick against. The game is also very fast, which means that any awarded free kick or kick-in must be taken within four seconds or the other team gets the ball.

Since FIFA did not want the new game with its divergent rules to be equated with outdoor football—known as "fútbol" in South America—and since many people were calling the new game “fútbol de salon,” the accepted label for the sport became an abbreviation of those two key words—“fútsal.” That has stuck ever since, and today the national leaders in fútsal are the same for men and women: number one, Brazil; number two, Spain; and number three, Portugal.

18

A United Nations of Soccer—in Kansas?

In the 1990s—after living in Chicago and before moving to Iowa, where we would raise our sons—my wife and I lived for eight years in Kansas, where we had first met. We resided in the college town of Manhattan, home of Kansas State University.

Kansas had changed much since the seventies, when I was a child in the northeast corner of the state. Around Doniphan County, soccer was considered an oddity, even ridiculed by friends who played football and basketball. Of course, I knew from my years in Chicago that soccer was becoming more known and accepted, but now that I was back in Kansas, I was curious what soccer-playing opportunities I would find.

On arrival, I already knew much about Manhattan since my father had grown up there and he and Mom had returned so that he could work at the university health center after their years in East Africa. In his youth, Dad would often walk five blocks to the limestone stadium on campus, a buff-colored stone fortress with toothed battlements, where the K-State Wildcats played American football against Big Eight teams such as the Jayhawks, the Cornhuskers, and the Sooners. As a result, I associated KSU with American football. However, after a few months of asking around, I was delighted to find a whole crew of soccer players gathering every Saturday and scrimmaging inside that same still-standing limestone stadium.

The players at those pickup games were mainly international

students but included other internationals who lived in the area for one reason or another plus a few experienced Anglo-Americans. After several years of playing with the group, I learned that the local parks and rec department was organizing an over-thirty soccer league, so I convinced some of the older fellows to form a team.

Summer in central Kansas is truly summer. The temperature from July through August can hit 100. We played anyway, thankful for the little strip of shade that formed in the late afternoon along the tree-lined western edge of the designated field. We dragged our substitute benches over there for relief, and sometimes we stayed afterward, drinking copious amounts of Gatorade as we recounted our exploits.

For six years, that team won every game, walking away with all the championship T-shirts to the chagrin of every other team. The league was small—only six or seven teams—and we played on reduced fields with only six players to a side, so this extended win streak was not a huge accomplishment. We were certainly not going to be recruited by the British Premier League, let alone a Major League Soccer team. However, it was still a satisfying string of victories, and I look back with fondness at the guys who played with me during those years, amazed now by how transnational we were, even in the heart of the Midwest.

Siendou, barely thirty, was a grad student in electrical engineering. He was from Côte d'Ivoire along the coast of western Africa. He had a stubbly beard and a quick, winsome smile, and he was a regular assassin once he got the ball, despite wearing a knee brace for a torn ACL. Pass him the ball once or twice, and you were almost guaranteed a goal.

Mustapha, from the coastal city of Dar es Salaam in Tanzania, was also a grad student and a bit older, maybe thirty-five. He was with us for four summers while working on a PhD in agricultural economics. In the winter, he would balloon a bit because of having no exercise, but as the summer wore on, he would become craggier and craggier. He was the sweetest, most cheerful fellow in conversation, but if you dribbled a ball into his defensive zone, you'd better be prepared for combat. He would not let you through without contact. Even after the league organizers banned slide tackles, he still couldn't help going into slides. They were the sort that would be permitted in a professional match, but they were so fierce that they almost always sent the dribbling forward flying, which then resulted in a near-riot by the other team.

Hugo, from Costa Rica, was *not* a grad student. He lived in town and worked for Pioneer Company as a seed researcher specializing in sorghum. He was pushing fifty and balding. Short and stocky, he couldn't run like the rest of us. In fact, he had one calf that was strangely deformed due to a bite from a brown recluse spider. He also missed games now and then because of kidney stones. In other words, Hugo seemed like less of a threat. But you didn't ignore him without consequences. He would show up quietly in the right place at the right moment, then make a quick little assisting pass or fire the ball home. And he had loads of confidence—so much, in fact, that if you didn't see him when he was open, he would explode, reminding you that he still existed and knew how to play the game, damn it!

Then there was Jorge from Mexico, who made his living as a commercial housepainter, sometimes reworking the interiors of whole office buildings, where he specialized in ceilings, spending whole days with stilts strapped to his legs. Because I had been a house painter in college, I knew how much energy was required to paint normal walls. All that stooping and straining and ladder lifting and sanding and repetitive brushing! But to add stilts and all the soreness that came from the straps and awkward walking? I was astounded. I couldn't believe how easily he hopped out of his pickup and then ran all over the soccer field, making smart, exact midfielder passes, not to mention exchanging jokes afterward and heading home to mow his lawn.

Others came and went, such as an effusive Brazilian or a videographer from Idaho who worked for the university. Finally, there was my brother Nat, who had gone through junior high and early high school with me, playing soccer in East Africa. Now he was working as a missionary in western Africa, but he was able to bring his family back to Kansas every other summer, when he would become a regular.

In Cameroon, Nat would travel with a local team to nearby villages, playing for pride, not much more. Winning brought notoriety to the community, so games were still hotly contested, and all sorts of efforts were made to assure success. On one occasion, the other team even buried fetishes by their goalposts to ward off the ball. Nat didn't believe the accusations until someone from his team actually dug up one of the fetishes.

In any case, Nat was seasoned, and we had a natural understanding, having played together for so long. While I might move up to midfield during those six-on-six games, where I could work with Jorge on setting up shooters, Nat and Mustapha could be counted on to stop anything that broke through our midfield line. On the flip side, if Nat or Mustapha made a sudden run forward, I knew instantly to drop back into the area they had vacated, preparing to slow possible counterattacks.

Jorge too had a clear sense of that interchangeableness, which meant the four of us were an organic, ever-evolving unit, working in sync to stop the ball and then to move it back downfield, sometimes even switching off with the forwards to make our own runs at the goal. I look back and chuckle because the ball got through to our own goal so rarely that we could actually take turns playing goalie, having no one truly designated for the position. In fact, sometimes we would pass the ball back to that bored player simply to keep him from feeling left out.

Finally, the summer came when I would have to leave Manhattan. My wife and I were moving to Iowa, where I would pursue another grad degree—this time an MFA in creative writing. I was forty, and our two sons were now four and eight. The team gathered one last time for a barbecue on the porch of Hugo's house, and just before we dug into the food, I told the guys I was feeling a bit hot, so I needed to take off a shirt. I was wearing a championship T-shirt from that very summer—2001—but under it was the shirt from 2000. I said, "You know, I'm still feeling kind of hot," so I peeled off another shirt, exposing the next one down—from 1999. And so I continued, removing five shirts in all until I got down to the original season of 1996.

Each of those championship shirts brought another round of delighted cheering. We had become not just a team but good friends. Yes, the wins meant a lot. But it meant more that we had done it together.

19
The Darker Side

Although soccer can be a very welcoming game, I know it has its darker side. And the trouble can begin at the earliest level, as I learned soon after I completed high school in Kenya and began college in suburban Chicago.

To make pocket money during those college years, I managed a Saturday soccer program for children in a parks-and-rec program of nearby Villa Park. This was in the early eighties, and since I was a penniless "missionary kid," I had no car. Instead of driving, I rode a bike six miles, arriving at 8 AM so I could set up the fields.

The kids were third and fourth graders, and most of them were completely inexperienced. Back in those soccer-as-novelty days, I was an "expert" of sorts. Otherwise, I doubt I would have been hired.

Anyway, I delivered cones and balls from a storage closet, then helped coaches run training drills before refereeing a game or two. For the most part, parents were simply glad to see their kids running around. At games, they cheered enthusiastically for any kid who did anything worth noting. As a ref, I only occasionally got guff from the sidelines, and only mild guff. However, there were exceptions.

One Saturday, a little dervish of a player raced right into a slower, overweight boy who was dribbling downfield. Because the little guy was slight, he bounced off, crashing to the ground.

He began to cry and had to be consoled before he would get back on his feet. Then I set the ball down in front of the larger boy for a free kick.

Yes, the smaller one had been hurt, but he was the one who'd committed the foul, so it seemed fair to award the kick to the child who had lost advantage. No matter, though. As soon as I indicated which direction we were kicking, a man started to bellow from the sidelines, "What the hell! That's not who got hurt."

I ignored the shouting while the bigger boy, nervous now, looked for assurance that he really *was* allowed this kick. I gave him a thumbs-up and blew the whistle. Then the kids resumed play. However, as I ran beside them, a red-faced forty-year-old in cargo shorts emerged from the crowd and strode down the sideline in step with me, yelling, "What's your problem, ref? Hey, I'm talking to you."

I still ignored him, hearing a coach call out, "Cool it, guy. These are just kids."

"Easy for you to say," the man yelled back. "It's not your son getting shafted."

I was only twenty years old and did not want to confront an older man in front of all these people, but now I could see that the children, hearing him, were becoming tentative about dribbling or passing, as if anything could be a mistake. Ironically, the boy who had committed the foul was the only one showing no caution. He dashed all over the field, chasing the ball from player to player, and though he got a toe on it once or twice, there was no sense of controlling it. He seemed bent on disruption, nothing more.

I whistled for everyone to stop, then walked a couple of steps toward the angry father. "Sir, I'm sorry your son got hurt, but he was the one who banged into the other player. That was the foul, so that's why—"

"I don't have to take this bullshit," he blurted out, "not from a college dipstick." He took a step onto the field, and I was very thankful to see both coaches close in, walking between him and me.

One of them murmured, "Hey, let the kids play, okay? Look at them. They just wanna play."

The man glared at this coach and glared at me. "I'm not forgetting this," he hissed. Then he pivoted and strode back into the crowd, which parted quickly.

I jogged over to a boy who had his foot on the game ball, and as I jogged, I could see the mad father striding across the empty field behind all the watching parents. Then I whistled for the kids to resume playing. Not until the game ended did I get a chance to thank the coach who had defused the situation, and that was when I got the full scoop. Apparently, the upset man was divorced and hated the boy's new stepfather. He hated the stepdad so much that he had taken to showing up unexpectedly, trying to intimidate him. Having heard that the stepfather had registered the boy for soccer, he had come to our field despite a restraining order. In fact, the stepfather had once confided that the other man, while drunk, had threatened to shoot him.

"To be honest," said the coach, "I didn't know whether he was leaving us or going to get a gun. The stepdad says he's got one in the glove compartment."

Soccer, for all its potential inclusivity, has its uglinesses. Like any sport, it can become a substitute for war. Old resentments take hold, triggering aggression. Whole teams get thrown off the rails and become belligerent due to one perceived injustice or due to incessant taunting from the sidelines. Sometimes a single fan—like that alienated father—will cause the havoc, and sometimes a single short-fused player triggers the trouble by bringing his personal issues onto the field.

During the year before I helped to form an over-thirty team in Manhattan, Kansas, I played for a season with a mostly African team connected to Kansas State University. This was a very good, younger team, strong enough to defeat the army team at nearby Fort Riley. In fact, we would have beaten them and won the league championship except for a single distrustful Nigerian teammate—a short, rock-hard guy who always felt discriminated against. He was so reactive toward supposed slights that during the deciding game he actually caused the referee to send us off the field and call it a forfeit.

This player, Victor, protested a single call by the referee, becoming so loud and adamant that the ref had to give him a red card. Then he refused to leave the field, stalking around beside the ref. He was so stubborn that he eventually took a stand on the middle line and threatened to fight anyone, including his own teammates, who were begging him to stop.

We had been winning that game handily—two goals to zero. The league title was ours if we could just finish what remained of the second half. But instead it went to those soldiers, and the rest of us came off the pitch completely frustrated. I stayed so frustrated that, a year later, in the middle of another deciding game, when the same guy went into a similar rant, I actually went to him and wrapped my arms around him, shouting, "Not again. There are other people out here, not just you."

I had considered Victor a friend throughout all of this. We had been on good terms. He would even tease me when I delivered a strong slide tackle, saying, "I didn't think you still had it in you." However, after he backed down that evening and after we went on to win the game, taking the league championship, he came up to me and said, "Don't you ever talk to me like that again."

We played together for another season or two, but Victor never again welcomed me or spoke to me warmly, staying resentful that I had slighted him in front of the other men on the team. When I pleaded with him to let it go, he insisted, "No, no. I can see the real you now." Even after I apologized for being so commanding,

I could not convince him I was still a friend, just an honest one.

Soccer is not all hugs and kisses, that's for sure. Players often bring their psychic flaws onto the field. In my case, it is a righteous indignation that flares when a player does something that seems mean-spirited or unfair, like grabbing a jersey and not letting go. That is the sort of thing that can cause me, despite being generally tolerant, to become aggressively physical, risking injury or a card from the referee.

Players have confrontational triggers no matter how high you go up the ladder. At the championship game of the 2006 World Cup in France, the French star Zinedine Zidane, who had scored the first goal, inexplicably turned and headbutted the Italian player Marco Materazzi, who had tied the game with an equalizing goal. Materazzi, after receiving this blow to his chest, fell to the ground writhing. This resulted in an instant red card and ejection for Zidane and contributed to the French loss, even though it became apparent that Materazzi had been goading Zidane, making ugly comments about his sister and mother.

There's also Luis Suárez, who infamously bit the shoulder of an opponent during a 2014 World Cup game.

And what about the fans who go ballistic, losing all perspective? One of the worst cases happened to poor Andrés Escobar, a Colombian defender who accidentally kicked a ball into his own goal during the 1994 World Cup. When Colombia was knocked out of the tournament, Escobar returned home, where he went to a bar and was accosted by two men who took out handguns and shot him six times.

The only bright side of that terrible incident is what happened next. Although Escobar had been vilified by fans all across Colombia, after the assassination his funeral was attended by more than 120,000 contrite mourners—people who could see just how wrong things had become.

DID YOU KNOW?
A Homeless World Cup

Every year since 2003, the Homeless World Cup organization has hosted a tournament that brings together homeless soccer teams from as many as sixty-four nations. The inaugural tournament took place in Graz, Austria, but since then, it has shifted annually, occurring in Gothenburg, Edinburgh, Copenhagen, Cape Town, Melbourne, Milan, Rio de Janeiro, Paris, Mexico City, and five other cities.

This street-ball version of soccer is played outdoors on turf the size of a basketball court, with only four players per team, including a goalie. Each game is a quick fourteen minutes in duration. The only other distinction is that all participating players must have been homeless in the previous year. In some cases, that means the player is still actively seeking political asylum. Others are in rehabilitation from drug or alcohol addiction. And some simply lost their homes when they were laid off at work.

The hands-down champion in both the men's and women's divisions of these homeless World Cups is Mexico. Even though no player can return after competing in the previous year, Mexico has fielded different winning teams four times for men and eight for women. The most recent win for the Mexican women was in 2023, when California hosted and the Mexican team defeated the Chilean team at Sacramento State Hornet Stadium.

20
Mr. Soccer–Oumar Seck

After leaving our home in Manhattan, Kansas, we spent twenty years in Iowa, where our sons came of age. Then Cathleen and I returned to Kansas, moving to Topeka, where I once again went looking for soccer players. I had to leave town to find a consistent pickup game, and that was in Lawrence, where I had gone to grad school. Soon after joining the group, I noticed one player in particular—a six-foot-four sturdy African man who was at least forty years old. I noticed him because, even though he was taller than others and considerably older, he played with confident grace.

If trapped by multiple defenders in a corner of the field, he didn't panic. He turned away calmly, protecting the ball with his body, then faked one direction but pivoted back, tapping the ball through the narrow gap he had created between the off-balance double-team. It all happened so smoothly and surely that it had a deceptive slow-motion feel. His little pass would spin to the foot of a waiting teammate but spin right back since he was already out of the defensive trap and gliding down the sideline with long-legged strides, ready to receive the ball again.

Months passed before I realized something that made me more curious about this towering man with calm moves and a raucous laugh that burbled out when he was receiving congratulations or jabs from good-natured opponents. I realized that one of the three women who played with us—a tall, dark-haired

Anglo—was his wife. Then I noticed that when she pulled up in their van, two teenage boys and a five-year-old would jump out in soccer gear and begin practicing on the end of our field. It seemed that, for this man, soccer was a family tradition, not just a solo activity.

Another thing I noticed—and it seemed a natural extension of his family approach to soccer—was that this fellow player showed no partiality about making passes. Some players are instinctively inclined toward favored teammates, either because they don't trust other players or because they are maintaining a kind of on-field friendship that matters to them more than how successful the scoring is. But Oumar—for that is the name I picked up eventually—had a generous manner that included whoever was the next logical person in an evolving play. If he passed to me, I sensed his unspoken trust, his implicit faith in the team, not just a few cronies.

In other words, Oumar played the way a coach should play—as if modeling the right moves with each decision. As a result, I was not surprised to learn that he was, indeed, a coach. A friend tipped me off over dinner. "You play with Oumar?" he asked. "That man's a legend. He coaches practically every Lawrence kid. My son had him too."

My friend went on to describe a particular moment that stayed with him from the years when his boy played for Oumar's club team through the Kaw Valley Soccer Association. A heated argument broke out on the sidelines at one of the high school matches, and the conflict was moving toward physical blows. However, as soon as the group saw Oumar tramping toward them—his tall, sturdy figure looming closer—every one of the young men went quiet and stepped back from their antagonists.

"He's the friendliest guy," said my friend, "but a friendly giant is still a giant!"

After that dinner conversation, I started to pay more attention when playing with Oumar, and I started to see just how wide an influence he had. Certain college-age players interacted with him so amiably and with such warm respect that I began to realize they were former protégés. Sam, who was one of the most adept strikers, would show up only during summer and winter holidays, coming home from where he played for Grinnell College in Iowa, but he always met Oumar with a big grin. Robert, who dribbled at lightning speed and sometimes chortled as he outmaneuvered me, had a cheerful deference toward Oumar, even though Robert had become a hired coach for the Lawrence high school team. Then there was Abdullah, who could dribble through an entire squad of defenders, putting an exclamation point on his zigzag attack by shooting a rocket into the goal. I saw him treating Oumar with the same friendly respect.

As I was teasing Oumar one day about all these disciples, having counted five or six on the field, I asked him where he had grown up, and I learned that he was from Senegal. Then he described some of his early life in Pikine, an arrondisement on the edge of the capital city, Dakar. His grandfather, the local imam, had a house next to the Pikine soccer stadium, which meant Oumar could go up on the roof and watch all the games. He did that constantly from April to November, and since his cousin Khadim was a star on the Pikine team, Oumar had an instant in with all the players who represented their suburb against other neighborhoods. If they gathered in a teahouse to boast about recent wins or to strategize in preparation for the next game, then Khadim would allow Oumar to sit next to him, absorbing all the soccer talk.

That's where his devotion to soccer really took root. "I tell you," he said with a chuckle, "I wanted to be as popular—no, more popular than Khadim." Then he lowered his voice confidentially, still grinning but with a touch of embarrassed vulnerability. "Honestly, though, I was the worst player in my family.

Even my father, who was the president of the Pikine club, didn't see much potential."

After laughing a big belly laugh, he explained that he was the youngest in a whole age group of cousins and siblings, which meant he often wasn't allowed to join their games. Instead, he had to go off and practice on his own, kicking a ball against a wall. He played street soccer with kids his own age, putting down bricks as goalposts and taking them back up if a car came rumbling through. Meanwhile, his cousin Khadim became noticed enough to receive an invitation from a Belgian professional team, which meant he traveled overseas, and that fueled Oumar's dreams more, making him eager to leave Senegal.

As he reached the last years of secondary school, Oumar began to beg his father to help him go to college overseas. He would become a pilot, he declared, having been impressed by a neighbor's snazzy airline uniform. So his father finally told him to apply. Canada was the first option, but it seemed awfully cold. The US had better music videos, which helped to swing the decision. Then he was accepted at three American universities and had to choose among them. Not knowing a thing about Michigan State University as compared with the University of Arizona or the University of Kansas, he asked a brother to write all three school names on slips of paper, and when he pulled one out of his brother's closed fist, it was KU.

Just being accepted into an American university was such an accomplishment that Oumar was not at all prepared for the realities that followed. Assuming that he could easily get around once he landed in the States, he booked a flight that went only to New York. He arrived midwinter, and when he stepped out of the sliding glass doors at John F. Kennedy Airport, he was so stunned by the frigid air that he had to retreat into the building and unpack multiple layers of shirts as a makeshift coat.

Oumar thought he would just take a bus to Kansas, having

always used buses in Senegal, but he had no idea it would take two days and nights to reach his destination, switching buses over and over as he made his way west to Cleveland, then Chicago, then Des Moines, then Kansas City until finally he was dropped off past midnight, exhausted and hungry, in a cold, dark lot outside a Lawrence gas station. A nearby hotel wouldn't take cash, and he didn't know how to get to another hotel until the kind receptionist called a taxi for him and pointed him to a hotel that *would* accept cash. When he finally lay down on the bed in that much-too-expensive room, he began to weep, thinking, *I don't know if I can do this*.

Oumar's father had told him before he got on the plane in Dakar, "Remember, we are still here. If you need to call, or even turn around, it's okay!" He desperately didn't want to fail in the bold decision that had cost his family so much, but his father's words came back to him now, and only two things kept him from making a call that might have changed the whole trajectory of his life:

1. When he walked into an initial orientation meeting at KU, he sat down next to two young Black men who turned out to be from Senegal and greeted him in his mother tongue, Wolof.
2. Within a few weeks, he found a group playing pickup soccer.

As soon as Oumar jumped in with that group of athletes playing on a field near the famous Allen Fieldhouse, where Phog Allen coached the initial KU basketball program to three national titles, he just felt free again—galloping around without a worry in his head. Here in the US, he was a stellar player, which meant he was noticed right away and recruited to play on the KU club team. That team excelled, doing so well that they traveled to their own national tournament, barely losing in the quarterfinals to the University of Virginia club team that would go on to win the US title.

Soon Oumar was flourishing in his new American life. However, he was also becoming aware that his studies at KU were costing an awful lot and that he did not have a clear career path after letting go of his whimsical interest in wearing a pilot's uniform. As a result, when the nearby Johnson County Community College offered him a free soccer scholarship, he transferred. Although he was enthusiastic about playing striker on a true collegiate team, he had to make a sudden unexpected adjustment. A key defender became injured, so his coach plugged him in at center backfield. Game after game, Oumar played defense even though it was not what he had hoped. Nevertheless, after the final game ended, the coach pulled him aside to say, "Oumar, I don't know if you realize what you have just done, but you managed somehow to play a full season in the backfield and still be our top scorer!"

During that single season, others noticed Oumar's ability as well, so he was recruited again, by MidAmerica Nazarene University in Kansas City, where he received another scholarship that would allow him to finish his college career. However, by the time he made that switch, he had also started a side job in Lawrence, where a Senegalese friend needed help with a burgeoning youth soccer program. While Oumar went on to win honors playing for MidAmerica Nazarene, it was on the practice fields with the youth players that he realized what he really wanted to do with his future. Once he was coaching all those young, eager players alongside a Brazilian boys' coach and a Dutch girls' coach, he felt that he had arrived home: "It just felt like this was what I was made to do."

That was in 2005, and Oumar has been coaching ever since, preparing young players for two full decades. He laughed as he recalled that midway through his first year of coaching, he surprised his early high school players with this question: "You all want to play college ball, don't you?" They looked at each other as if Oumar had just said, "You want to colonize Mars, don't you?" Apparently, no one from the Kaw Valley Soccer Association had made a jump into college soccer yet. However, by the time that group graduated, six had signed with college teams, a trend that has continued every year since, expanding to not just Kansas-based schools but also colleges in Texas, Illinois, Colorado, Washington, and Missouri. Out of ten seniors in the most recent group, seven signed with college teams.

When Oumar strolls onto yet another immaculate turf pitch in Texas or Iowa, where he travels with his Kaw Valley Soccer teams, how far it must seem from the dusty streets where he used to practice with his siblings, setting up bricks as goalposts. And how removed from the rooftop perch where he watched his cousin become famous in the Pikine stadium or the teahouses where they would meet afterward to "talk football." But when he walks out there with his youth team from Kansas, he does it proudly. "My 'jambars,'" he calls them, which is Wolof for "warriors."

21
Football to Fútbol

I had a friend years ago who worked in a meatpacking plant in Emporia, Kansas. He had one of the most awful jobs imaginable. Because Japanese customers prized cattle intestines, he spent all day blowing shit out of those tubelike guts. I don't mean with his lips—like a trumpet—but it almost seemed that bad when he described the job.

Each of the coiled intestines, heavy with excrement, had to be fitted—at one end—onto a high-pressure blower and then clamped in place until a blast of water straightened it out and sent the contents flying. As I recall, this high-velocity manure splattered into a bin, but sometimes the flexing intestine thrashed like a loose fire hose, spraying in unpredictable directions.

Mark, of course, wore a full-body plastic suit not unlike the hazmat outfit at a toxic waste site. Nevertheless, when he unzipped and stepped out for lunch break, he did not find coworkers lining up to share his table. His work was not just filthy but lonely, and though he made me laugh uncontrollably when describing how shit literally "hit the fan," I have been haunted by the story ever since.

Here's the thing, though. Tens of thousands of workers are still employed by meatpacking businesses across the Midwest, not just in Emporia but also in southwest Kansas communities such as Dodge City, Liberal, and Garden City. Some, like Mark, are blasting feces out of intestines, but others are doing work that is nearly as messy or odoriferous and often more hazardous. The "knocker" is firing a bolt gun into skulls of panicked cows, killing over 2,500 a day. Others are skinning hanging carcasses, getting smeared by blood and dung. Some are dropping animal corpses into scalding vats with superheated water or sawing through flesh and bone with electric saws or slicing away meat from ribs or dumping strips of beef into a huge vat with spinning blades that will create hamburger. They are spending eight to twelve hours a shift dismantling the bodies of cows as fast as they can, with blades that are constantly moving, constantly at risk of slipping and cutting their own bodies, and they are doing it for about $18–20 per hour.

These are not prime jobs for most Americans, who would prefer not to wear soiled plastic slickers and splattered face shields all day or to listen to high-volume iTunes to drown out the endless racket of whirring saws and clanking conveyors. As a result, more than 45 percent of meatpacking workers are foreign-born immigrants who cannot get better jobs due to limited English or a lack of connections. If you add the second-generation offspring who continue in this line of work, over half of meatpackers are from immigrant families.

In parts of southwest Kansas, that reality means certain historically white communities have received huge influxes of foreign residents, primarily from Mexico or Central America but now from Africa and Asia as well. And along with the unfamiliar languages or foods that these newcomers bring to the area comes a foreign-seeming sport: soccer.

That's a pretty big deal if you think about it, since rural white communities in Kansas have been historically devoted to American football, along with basketball and baseball. Such all-American sports have reigned supreme in the heartland. But suddenly the children of immigrants are flooding certain Kansas grade schools and high schools, and they are, by their sheer numbers, creating a shift in the sporting culture.

The original spike in Spanish-speaking residents in southwest Kansas took off in the 1990s, when the labor demand was rising rapidly at meatpacking plants, and today the population of Latinx people in just one community—Garden City—is over 65 percent. Nevertheless, at first there was little interest from Garden City High School administrators in the new sport that arrived with the migrants. Nothing came of it until a Mexican-born guidance counselor at Garden City High School, Joaquin Padilla, began a boys' soccer team in 1996 and then a girls' team in 2000.

The fledgling programs floundered initially, largely due to turnover. Parents would stay only for a season, moving on to other jobs, and Padilla would have to rebuild his teams. The kids had no reason to be proud either. At first, they had no uniforms, so they had to buy matching T-shirts. Only one or two players had cars, so they would have to pack into those cars to get to practice. And when they played official games, they were lucky if twenty fans showed up, compared to the hundreds who came to football and basketball games.

Elbin Palencia, who was one of the early soccer players at Garden City High, recalls that Coach Padilla pushed back against the low self-esteem he saw in those first players. "Sometimes I have to say it frustrated him when he saw kids on his team with really a low feeling about what their possibilities were and what they wanted to accomplish in life. It bothered him enormously that a lot of them, their great dream was to get out of high school and go to work in the meat plants for $13 an hour."

Another player, Rey Ramirez, recalls, "I don't remember him solely pushing soccer. He was more thinking of us as an individual, as a person for a future, going to school, going to college."

In any case, the Garden City boys' team began to win some

key games in 2003, and a shift began to take place. Sam Quinones, who has written about the remarkable growth that followed, was interviewed for the documentary *From Football to Futbol*, and he says, "You began to see kinda an awakening on the part of the student body and therefore on the part of the players themselves. They began to feel a bit better about themselves, walk a little bit taller . . . They were being slapped on the back by the teachers as they walked through the hallways, and students would put up newspaper stories of their last game."

In that pivotal year of 2003, before the last game of the season, the Garden City High School held a pep rally for the boys' soccer team—the first pep rally for anything that seemed Latinx, according to Quinones. "This was reserved," he observes. "This was solely for the football team. Kinda a secular mass or something like that. They would come through this big inflated tunnel, and all the students would be packing the gym. This was the first time when it was held for a soccer team. They came out of the big tunnel and the kids are screaming. The band's blasting. It was just this beautiful inspirational moment. The kind you see in Hollywood movies."

Elbin Palencia recalls running out of that tunnel into the cheering crowd: "At that moment, I didn't see color. I just saw like one high school being united and being supportive."

They played their first game of the state tournament soon after. It was at home but in terrible weather—cold and rainy. Nevertheless, three hundred fans came to watch. At first, the boys were intimidated by the mere appearance of their opponents, who were from Maize High School near Wichita—tall, strong guys with expensive cleats and matching gym bags and windbreakers. The Garden City guys huddled in the cold, wearing thin jerseys or mismatched jackets. Some had scanned the Maize team website, seeing that the opposing players were profiled with a kind of soccer résumé and a list of traveling games and tournaments.

they had won. "And we were just Garden City, man," recalls Rey Ramirez. "I mean, we were not anything more than that."

Somehow, though, they gained enough confidence to hold off the initial Maize attacks and to settle into the game, playing it the way they wanted. At the end of regulation time, the score was tied, so it stretched into overtime then double overtime. Finally, they had to go to penalty kicks. After the usual five paired shots, they were still tied, so they had to go to sudden-death kicks. On the seventh kick, the other team missed, so they knew they could finally win—if only they made the next shot. And Elbin was the player who had the honor of firing the ball into the left corner just under the outstretched hands of the Maize goalie.

Coach Padilla, looking back at that major win, the first of many that would follow, says, "They competed not only with the teams externally but competed with themselves internally." In his opinion, the inner win is what mattered most. Although they would *not* go on to win the state championship, they had proven themselves as members of the Garden City community, becoming integrated in a way that had not been possible before.

"Garden City, it loves us, and we love it," says Rey Ramirez. "And a lot of things happened that . . . we didn't think were possible. I think that's something I take away—just that it is possible, anything that you strive for. And I think that, for the most part, for the immigrant's mindset, that's not the case. You feel limited, like you don't know, like you're not capable. That year showed us the opposite of that, you know, and that we are not inferior."

Certainly, Garden City soccer players have continued to show they are not inferior, competing well at the state level even though they must play against more-advantaged teams from suburban Kansas City, Topeka, Wichita, and Lawrence. In fact, twenty years after that landmark 2003 season, they were back in the quarterfinals of the state championship, playing against

Washburn Rural High School from Topeka and barely losing in overtime.

This phenomenon is not limited to Garden City either. In neighboring Dodge City, a similar tradition has taken root due to soccer-playing youth from meatpacking families. The players have names such as López and García and Macías and Castillo, and they have won the boys' State Championship twice, in 2016 and 2020, going undefeated both seasons. As for the girls' teams, in the most recent season, Garden City became the regional champion after defeating the Manhattan High School team and moving on to the state quarterfinals.

In some sense, these young men and women, almost all of them from Spanish-speaking immigrant families, are bringing history full circle. What many may not realize is that before 1848 and the defeat of the Mexican army, the southwest corner of Kansas was actually *part* of Mexico, as was the Oklahoma Panhandle and all of Texas plus New Mexico and a large part of Colorado. The first white settlers to come to southwest Kansas came because of a fort built to protect the Santa Fe Trail, which was a trading route between the US and Mexico with hundreds of oxcarts passing every week. And even after the loss of all that northern territory, Mexican cowboys—known as vaqueros—were still active as part of the major cattle drives that brought Texas longhorns to Kansas to be shipped to slaughterhouses in Kansas City and beyond.

The vaqueros and their cattle traditions were present from the start in the cattle-ranching culture of the Midwest. Those indigenous cowboys braided their own ropes and designed chaps to protect against bristling chaparral. The word "lasso," in fact, is based on the Spanish term for rope, "lazo."

So the supposed foreignness of meatpacking families from south of the US border is actually a bit misleading here in Kansas. Once Mexican vaqueros roamed the whole area, and their cattle-ranching traditions helped to shape the Kansas ranches that exist today. Soccer wasn't their thing back then, but it is now, and since they have become a part of modern Kansas, soccer is more and more of a Kansas thing as well!

DID YOU KNOW?

Why International Games are Called Caps

International appearances are called "caps" in soccer. Why?

Because in the early days in England, where the game was being standardized, a player who represented the nation at an international game was given an old-fashioned hat with a short bill that poked out over the forehead (much like early-era baseball caps).

The original caps, awarded to English players back in 1886, were white silk with an embroidered red rose on the front. Since no one had invented a soccer jersey, they had a practical purpose too, not just symbolic: they helped to identify teammates during games.

Today, physical caps may not be as customary, but when a player reaches one hundred games for his or her national team, that player is often awarded an actual cap to commemorate the accomplishment. The male player with the most international caps might be a surprise: it's Soh Chin Ann from Malaysia, who played for fifteen years from 1969 to 1984 and earned 219 caps. For women players, the honor goes to American striker Kristine Lilly, who played for twenty-three years from 1987 to 2010, competing in five World Cups and eventually earning a whopping 354 caps.

22

Building Soccer Bridges

When our eldest son turned fourteen, I received a travel grant as a writer. That meant I could afford to take Conrad with me on a trip to Kenya, where he could see a bit of my other "homeland." He would also get to hang out with several cousins, since my brother Nat was now working in Nairobi, providing services to the blind and deaf of East Africa.

Conrad and I traveled first to Lamu Island, off the coast of Kenya, where we learned about fourteenth-century Arab sea traders who built homes from chiseled coral, erecting one of the first mosques on the sub-Saharan coast. We toured the famous carved doors of the island, with their intricate geometric designs and Quranic inscriptions. We walked through a tall, crenellated fort built by an Omani sultan. We even went fishing from a wooden dhow, using baited hooks on a string that had to be reeled in on a block of wood.

Later, Conrad and I joined Nat's family in Nairobi and took a side trip to the Nakuru game park, where Conrad showed himself to be an adept "monkey whisperer," sitting cross-legged on the grass under an acacia and feeding vervets as they swung down to pluck pieces of candy bar from his hand. The smallest of the monkeys squatted and stared at him with hazel eyes and a dark, somber face ringed by white fur, and I loved how Conrad waited quietly, murmuring assurances, until the creature trusted him and took a few last steps.

All this was wonderfully memorable. But I find it interesting that I have equally vibrant memories from a brief side trip on the way back to Nairobi, when the Range Rover bumped and swayed up the escarpment to the boarding school where Nat and I had lived for two years as teens. So much came sweeping back to me as we arrived at the open, treeless soccer pitch with its majestic view of the immense Rift Valley. This was where I had played alongside friends from Canada and Australia and Kenya and Ethiopia, becoming skilled enough finally to earn "Most Improved" soccer player at the honors assembly. And what stays most from that visit back to Rift Valley Academy is an odd game of soccer that I joined.

My brother's kids, just like mine, had to have a soccer ball wherever they went, so they pulled it out of the Range Rover as soon as we arrived. We all passed it back and forth as we walked the school grounds, and when we came upon an empty concrete racquetball court, we simply couldn't resist taking the ball into that space. At first, we mimicked racquetball rules, serving by booting the ball to the end wall, then taking turns snapping it back to the end wall before it could bounce twice. After a bit, though, two junior high students came by—a Kenyan boy and his Anglo buddy—and since they stopped to watch, we invited them to join. The rules had to change, so we formed teams of three, turning the boxlike court into a very small, very crowded soccer field. We used shirts as goal markers, and all sorts of crazy ricocheting shots ensued, with echoing yells and everyone laughing in red-faced delight.

In the middle of it all, my son spun happily on the dusty concrete, sliding to a stop when necessary. And though I was just as engaged as he was, my deepest pleasure came from simply seeing him blend into that new ad hoc goofy game. I kept tapping the ball to others, keeping them in the action, because I could see how the game was allowing Conrad and his cousins to connect with complete strangers. Those other boys were from very different places than we were. Who knew where they had grown up or what lives they had led? But we were part of the same clan now—all of us happily surprised by our shared love of soccer. In some sense, that brief, playful connection trumped even the game park and exotic island that Conrad and I had visited, making us more present in Kenya than any touring we could do.

As it turned out, while Conrad and I were having such adventures in Kenya, Cathleen went traveling in England with our younger son, wanting him to have his own adventure, which meant that Conrad and I also got time with them on our way back from the father-son trip. The four of us stayed for a few nights with friends just across the bay from Plymouth, the famous port where a group of English Puritans set sail on the *Mayflower*, headed to the "New World."

In this Cornish corner of Britain, there were no vervet monkeys or houses built of coral and no people speaking Swahili. But everything was still foreign, as was evident with every jaunt we took. One afternoon, we rode a double-decker bus down narrow, hedged lanes to a coastal village thirty minutes away, where we could still see Plymouth across the bay. Cawsand was the name of the village, and we swam on the rocky beach, then ate fish and chips in a hotel pub that loomed over the breaking surf, atop a sturdy twenty-foot-tall seawall.

After lunch, we wandered to a tiny village square that was paved and had a compact granite monument at its center, a bit like an elongated chess pawn crowned by a polished stone ball. Maybe that granite sphere was our inspiration, but when we ducked into the little Shop on the Square, where one could buy flip-flops and beach toys, we noticed a very cheap soccer ball for sale, and the next thing I knew, my sons and I were out on the pavement dribbling and juggling.

Cathleen watched from a table at the shop, licking her ice

cream, and an elderly English couple grinned from another table across the square, next to the Cross Keys Inn. When the ball sprang loose and rolled to them, the man tapped it back, singing "Cheerio," and I thanked him, amused by the chalked message on a blackboard behind him: "Dogs Welcome in Bar, But If Wet Please Ask for Towels."

An occasional car sidled into the lazy intersection, halting our play. But this was a weekday, and the concrete square was generally free of traffic, so I felt comfortable stepping away eventually, joining Cathleen on her bench, where she handed me a bottle of ginger beer. We watched as the boys went on trapping and passing the ball, surprised when two local lads chased down an errant kick. Instead of simply taking the ball back, Conrad said a word or two and passed the ball to one of those boys, who trapped it underfoot and sent it rolling to Luke, who trapped it and sent it to the other boy, and suddenly our sons were hanging out with two English kids whom they would never have met if not for soccer.

By inviting two strangers into their game, our sons were once again bridging cultures, becoming just a little bit more connected to a new and intriguing society. In fact, they were beginning a connection that would still be very much alive twenty years later, when they were avid Arsenal fans, watching Premier League games in unison every weekend even though they lived a thousand miles apart—in Boston and Des Moines.

They were strengthening a bond that had also begun with their cousin Sebastian, who would come of age in Kenya, then serve in the Peace Corps in Nepal and later fall in love with a Spanish-speaking woman whose mother had immigrated to the US from Colombia. They were beginning a bond that would be evident even on the day of Sebastian's wedding rehearsal, when they would turn on the hotel TV to watch Arsenal play Brighton, retaking the lead in the Premier League. And this bond would be shared by Conrad's wife, from Turkmenistan, and Luke's girlfriend, a political organizer trying to bring an end to the terrible obliteration of people and homes in besieged Gaza.

Out there on that little patch of concrete in Cornwall, with the granite ball lifted overhead and two Cornish boys as playmates, my sons were essentially opening themselves to the world at large, and that took some risk. Rejection was possible, along with misunderstanding. However, by engaging with those two Cornish lads, Conrad and Luke were developing a receptivity that would serve them well in the future. Seated twenty yards away, sipping a soda with Cathleen, I felt more connected to both of them as a result—and proud!

23
A Family Affair

Both of my brothers, Nat and John, have played soccer with me over the years in all sorts of situations. Because John went to college while Nat and I returned to Ethiopia in the seventies, we didn't get to play with him as much, but then he joined us in South Sudan, where we enjoyed games in the dusty village of Doro. And after we came back from overseas, John would often help to gather international students at Kansas State University, where he had started graduate studies, so that the three of us could jump into pickup games during summer holidays.

Eventually, we each got married and began having kids, and something new happened—an expansion of our soccer tradition! Since we, as fathers, liked soccer so much, our children were inclined to join us—all five boys and two girls. If we pulled a ball out of the trunk on shared vacations and started to kick it around a parking lot or lawn, the children would scramble into action, glad (if nothing else) to play keep-away.

One summer when Nat was back from his new job in West Africa, where he was providing support for the blind and their families, we enrolled five of our growing kids in a British Soccer Camp run by young men and women with expert-sounding Scottish accents, who put our young charges through a week of skill-developing drills. This was happening in Kansas on blazing July days, and the two youngest boys, only four years old, were barely big enough to carry their water bottles, but they gamely ran the drills with older kids and took great pride in what they accomplished during end-of-practice scrimmages.

That was a start, and before we knew it, we had children playing with rec-league soccer teams, then joining school teams or soccer clubs. I even began coaching my sons' teams.

No wonder, then, that whenever we got all three families together, it became a habit to go looking for a field where we could play uncles against kids. To stay competitive, John, Nat, and I had to keep moving to new angles, looking for an open shot by shifting our passing triangle, but eventually the kids became savvy to what we were doing. They also became bigger and quicker and skilled enough to intercept our passes, dashing past our large, lumbering bodies, which meant it was time to break up the uncle coalition and start forming balanced teams.

Other families got pulled into our soccer orbit too. One summer, my cousin David visited from Washington, DC, with his two daughters, and we convinced the three of them to join us in a park near my parents' Kansas home. Afterward, everyone was so flushed and exhausted by the Kansas heat that we had to cool off in the shade for half an hour before dragging our sweaty, nearly cramping bodies back to cars and home.

Lots of memorable games took place as the years passed, such as a snow game our clan played against the clan of our Episcopal bishop, who was originally from England. We had just eaten a huge meal of Thanksgiving turkey and mashed potatoes, but for a zany hour, we slipped around in the cold, exhaling foggy gusts. My wife even joined the fun, trying to defend against the very athletic bishop, who was essentially her boss now that she was dean of the Des Moines cathedral. At one point, she raised an alarmed hand over her face, blocking an out-of-control bullet from the bishop. Then she shook her hand in pain, joking about an imagined newspaper headline—"Bishop Attempts to Murder Soccer-Playing Priest." In fact, a week later, she learned that a finger had been broken, which quickly made that Thanksgiving snow game even more legendary for our extended family.

I think, however, that perhaps the most unforgettable of all those family games was one that we played at the campus of the college in Michigan where brother John was a professor. He had somehow gotten his hands on a set of retired jerseys from the school's official soccer team, which he handed out in advance. This meant eight of us donned matching burgundy shirts as we took the field against six college students. We had them outnumbered, but they were all twentysomething, whereas we were either over forty or, in several cases, still in grade school. The hand-me-down jerseys looked awfully tight on Nat and John and me but hung like dresses on my ten-year-old son, Luke, and his slender cousin Alex.

Claire, our oldest, was halfway through high school, and she took a position on defense alongside me. It was a delight to watch her face up to those older students, physically blocking the lanes where they wanted to run, even if it meant collisions. She was only five feet tall, but she gamely set herself against them, stabbing her foot out in front of their passes and not flinching if she had to block a hard shot. Then she fired the ball to one of the other kids, perhaps her little brother, Alex, or her long-legged, galloping cousin Joanna.

Together, we would try to move the ball upfield toward fourteen-year-old Sebastian, who was still in junior high but the most talented of our kids. Sebastian was still short like his sister Claire, but he was a dribbling wonder, and he had a tenaciousness that would not be denied. He could maintain possession even against two of their defenders, and if he got entangled with them, he became like a threatened wolverine, legs scrabbling, body twisting, feet scooping until he emerged again with the ball.

The college students pulled ahead, as might be expected, but as a result of Sebastian's determination and our smart passing, we stayed close. And because Sebastian finally frustrated one guy a bit too much with an aggressive feet-whirling steal, the fellow shoved him right off the field and down a long embankment, where he tumbled into a grassy ditch.

As I recall now, Sebastian bounced right back up that ten-foot slope as if nothing had happened, and we played on. We didn't win, but when we walked away wearing our burgundy "Team Bascom" jerseys, the kids were all chattering about how well we had done, and of course, they were already forming another family soccer legend—"Remember the game when we were almost beating those college guys, and they got so mad they shoved Sebastian down a hill?"

As a family, we have had every reason to *not* stay together over the years. Nat moved his family to Mali, Cameroon, Uganda, and then Kenya. John's family has been situated ten hours away, sometimes spending a year overseas on academic sabbaticals. And Cathleen and I have kept moving every five or six years, living in six different towns or cities. Furthermore, there has been an ongoing diaspora with the younger generation, as different cousins have taken turns living as far away as Senegal, Nepal, Zambia, and Japan.

Nevertheless, when everyone comes back together again, someone will inevitably bring a soccer ball into the gathering, prompting short, quick passes in the living room or a pickup game at K-State's old stadium or a goofy session of "foot golf" on a golf course with holes the size of washtubs.

They say a family that plays together stays together, and if you ask our crew, I think they will heartily agree, happily recalling the games I have described plus a dozen others. At the center of them all? A soccer ball!

DID YOU KNOW?

War, Soccer, and a Surprising Truce

Some say soccer is war. However, on Christmas Day in 1914, it was a badly needed break *from* war. In West Flanders, Belgium, troops from Germany and England were hunkered down in muddy trenches, shivering and miserable. They had been like that for weeks, blasting away at each other with only a hundred yards of cratered, bullet-spattered earth between them. When they dared to lift a head, they could see frozen corpses. Then something unexpected happened.

One British officer, Peter Jackson, described it this way: "Somebody from the trench punted across a short football [that] landed amongst the Germans and they immediately kicked it back amongst our men. I spoke to the German officer and suggested that we have a football match. After a while he relented, and the match began."

Interviewed half a century after that remarkable, spontaneous game, Jackson recalled, "They were kicking the ball backwards and forwards to the trenches, to the barbed wire, for quite half an hour, until unfortunately the ball got impaled on one of the stakes of the barbed wire and was deflated."

Even a single impromptu game of that nature deserves mention in history books, but in fact, on that Christmas Day in 1914, numerous games broke out along a twenty-mile stretch of the World War I war zone. Another British veteran named Ernie Williams remembered his game this way: "From somewhere, somehow, this football appeared. [Then the Germans] took off their coats and put them down as goalposts. No referee; we didn't need a referee for that kind of game. It was like playing as a kid in the streets, kicking the ball about. . . . There was no score, no tally at all—it was simply a melee." Elsewhere, a unit of Scottish solders created goals with hats and played their enemies quite happily until finally halted by an upset German officer.

One of the great surprises of these unplanned, ad hoc games was that enlisted men rather than officers often initiated the action. To allow soldiers to take the lead was to abandon the chain of command. It could humanize the enemy as well, which risked diminishing the will to fight.

For reasons such as those, some refused to participate. For instance, a young corporal named Adolf Hitler stayed in the trenches, convinced the games were disgraceful.

Many did participate, though. And one soldier wrote home, saying, "Everybody on each side walked out to the middle of the two firing lines and, shaking hands, wished each other a Merry Christmas." Private Williams, looking back, said, "Everybody seemed to be enjoying themselves. There was no sort of ill will."

24
Bishops with Balls

In 2018, when we moved back to Kansas from Iowa, my wife became the first woman bishop of the Episcopal Diocese of Kansas, and four years later, all bishops of the Anglican ilk, which includes Episcopalians, met for the Lambeth Conference in Canterbury, sixty miles east of London. I got to come along, which is why I can now claim to be one of the very few soccer players who has played a soccer match with four New Zealand bishops.

A little background first. Bishops of the Anglican Communion gather every ten to twelve years at Canterbury because Anglicanism began in England, and the archbishop of Canterbury is the traditional overseer. This is still true, even though Anglicans are now spread across 160 nations worldwide, with the largest population being from the continent of Africa.

In any case, seven hundred bishops came to this Lambeth Conference, all of them staying in dorms at the University of Kent, and they were accompanied by an additional five hundred spouses. Meetings were long and monolithic. I felt small, sometimes intimidated by the linguistic and cultural differences. But after a week of sitting indoors, it occurred to me that I needed exercise, and that led me to approach complete strangers in purple clergy shirts and white collars, shyly asking if they played soccer.

This was a very mixed conference, with towering South Sudanese bishops and stout Latin American bishops plus an array of Asian, Pacific Island, European, and North American bishops that featured (for the first time) more than one hundred elected women. Given the international nature of the Anglican Communion, which has spread wherever the British Empire spread, many of these bishops had played soccer in their youth. But my problem was that bishops do not tend to be young anymore. Finally, at an outdoor dinner, while seated at a table with a man who looked to be a "youthful" forty, I found a possible recruit. Bishop Steve was from Kenya. He had emigrated to New Zealand and been elected there. He was, like many Kenyans, a devout cross-country runner, but when I timidly asked if he played soccer, he lit up.

Would he, perhaps, help to gather a crew of bishops and spouses for a game?

"Absolutely. I can think of at least three other bishops who will play—all from New Zealand."

Encouraged, I approached another dozen bemused bishops. Then I took my request to the spouses. In fact, I convinced Caroline Welby, wife of the archbishop, to make an announcement to all five hundred spouses.

Very British and very proper, Mrs. Welby looked startled when I introduced the idea of a pickup soccer match, but she gamely alerted the crowd of mostly sixty-year-old women, being sure to use the British term "football." My only taker? A sixty-five-year-old named Tom from Ontario, who served as a choirmaster in his wife's diocese and who was, apparently, a lapsed footballer. Tom was so enthusiastic about playing that he promptly went searching in the maze of tourist shops at the old city center until he had found and bought a lonely soccer ball.

Momentum was forming, sort of. I turned now to the only other source of players I could think of—the international work-study students who were stuck on campus for the summer, serving in the cafeteria. After a few awkward queries, I recruited two cautiously intrigued fellows—a tall, quiet Ukrainian and a very short, cheerful Ethiopian. Enough, at last, for a game of four-on-four.

Now, where to play?

We could simply occupy an empty lawn on the campus, avoiding the humps and holes of the scattered rabbit warrens, or I could try to get us onto one of the official campus pitches with their smooth artificial surfaces and permanent lines. The latter seemed "special" and certainly less conspicuous, so I went to inquire about reservations.

When I found the right athletic manager, he raised an eyebrow, having never encountered a sixty-year-old American who wanted to orchestrate a football match involving bishops. He was half my age and dressed in black polyester warm-ups. He had on a pair of indoor Adidas soccer shoes. And me? I was in khaki slacks, a button-down shirt, and slip-on dress shoes.

"Do your lads have boots?" he wanted to know.

"No, but we can use tennis shoes."

He paused. "Turf can be slippery."

"I've played on it in tennis shoes. We won't be going hard." Then, after waiting a beat, I added, "Just passing the ball a bit. Taking a break from meetings."

He gazed back, then smiled. "Sure, why not? We open our workout rooms to conference goers, so why not the pitches?"

So that was how the game finally became reality.

Unfortunately, on the evening itself, my fellow bishop-spouse, Tom, did not show up, which meant he didn't bring the ball he'd purchased in the tourist shop. However, the sports manager was there to unlock the gate, and he brought out a big netted bag of balls. Then the two international students wandered in.

Bishop Steve showed up next with his three large, middle-aged New Zealand colleagues. All of these conscripts were in their fifties, and I was surprised that one was the eccentric bishop my wife and I had noticed walking everywhere barefoot.

This ruddy-faced man with ropy dreadlocks had stayed unshoed, whether in the meeting rooms or on campus paths. He had glared when I stared too closely as he boarded the bus for a visit to the archbishop's dinner reception. He had even padded barefoot into the cathedral at the high church worship service, unfazed by the seven hundred other robed-and-shoed bishops, the phalanx of Catholic cardinals in skullcaps, and the column of orthodox patriarchs in black hatbox head coverings, who created a combined parade so long and solemn that forty minutes passed while they entered the building.

In other words, he had seemed like such an outlier that I did not think he would fit in with a group playing an organized sport, even as casual as this one. I was surprised to see him step onto that turf pitch, and I was even more surprised when he pulled on a pair of tennis shoes. Apparently, soccer allowed a break from his barefoot, monastic discipline.

Since Bishop Steve and I had called the group together, we took opposite sides and tried to form equal teams. Without spouse Tom, we had only seven players, so we decided to have one roving offensive player who would switch sides to play with whoever possessed the ball. The Ethiopian student seemed a likely candidate, and though he found the explanation confusing, he accepted the assignment with a wry smile. Then Steve gave me two of the New Zealand bishops, keeping a third for his team along with the quiet Ukrainian.

We started to play, and two things became quickly apparent: (1) Steve was very competitive, and (2) the bishops on my side, which included our usually shoeless cleric, were more skilled than either of Steve's players. This meant that when we gained possession and were joined by the roaming Ethiopian, we riddled their defense.

Bishop Steve, who had been smack-talking from the beginning, was running harder and harder as this lopsided game progressed, drawing on his long-distance stamina but struggling to stay Christian. His team kept fumbling the ball, falling behind 3–1 then 5–1, until finally, thank God, the bishops on my team recommended a break. They had remembered, it would seem, that the meek inherit the earth.

While resting, we shuffled teams, and after that reorganization, Bishop Steve scored a goal and ran to midfield in fist-pumping celebration. My team scored two goals, but his scored one more, and after ten minutes of a deadlocked tie, we collectively realized that this was the perfect time to end. Tired and satisfied, everyone plunked down on the turf in a sweaty cluster, laughing as I shouted that I wanted a photo.

By the time I had fetched the sports manager from the clubhouse and handed him my cellphone, the dreadlocked bishop had taken off his short-lived footwear. He was red-faced but no longer severe, instead chuckling. In the resulting photo, his sturdy, callused feet are planted solidly as he stands to one side in cutoff jeans. Bishop Steve, in the center, has his arms folded across the ball, and his legs are spread in a cocky, I-played-pretty-good stance. Meanwhile, the young guy from Ethiopia, whose name I unfortunately cannot remember, is looking to Steve and has his hand on top of the cradled ball, as if blessing it, and tall Andre, from Ukraine, is off to the side with an arm over the shoulder of that fellow work-study student.

All of us are smiling in the unintentional way that speaks of inner pleasure, not forced cheer, but what strikes me, as I look back at the photo, is the happy grin of Andre from Ukraine. He is so clearly enjoying our camaraderie. One would never guess that his family was stuck in a country that had been violently invaded five months earlier, that he didn't have any way to return home until the war was settled, or that he called his mother by cell phone weekly to make sure everyone was still alive. One would not guess, either, that he had allowed himself to play this game with bishops despite harboring a deep resentment toward orthodox patriarchs back home, who had been corrupted by money, in his opinion, and skewed by their relationship to the Russian Orthodox Church.

All this he would admit to me as we walked back at dusk toward the dorm where I stayed and where he, as an international student worker, served meals. He was so clearly glad just to have a bit of unexpected connection here in a foreign place—a free and open acceptance from strangers—that when we parted in the dormitory parking lot, this shy, reserved Eastern European reached out to give me an awkward but firm hug.

25
Reasons We Watch

2001: At the massive Mile High Stadium in Denver, which is normally jammed with fans of American football, so few Major League Soccer fans have come to see the Colorado Rapids that we can sneak right down—with our scalped tickets—to the fifth or sixth row, where all the die-hard supporters keep slowly chanting, "KoooooBeeeee," trying to distract the L.A. Galaxy star Cobi Jones. He is entirely unfazed, this dreadlocked midfielder who still, today, has played more international games for the US than any other: 164.

The Galaxy will go on to win not only that game but also the 2002 MLS Cup. However, what stays with me from that game is not a strike on goal or a saving dive by the goalie or anything else but my two blond sons, nine and five years old, grinning mischievously as they smack together the inflated tubes I bought for them, adding to the infernal gunshot noises that echo across the soccer pitch.

They whack those rigid tubes together, then join gleefully with the long-drawn-out chant—"KooooBeeeee!" For them, this way of watching is pure delight.

1994: A sea of blue-and-white faces is somewhat startling at Soldier Field in Chicago when I enter to watch Greece vs. Bulgaria during the group stage of the World Cup. It would seem that all 150,000 Chicago Greeks are here, eager to celebrate their Old

World origins. They roar as the game starts, full of hope. Then they groan as Bulgaria scores. They roar again when a striker breaks free and almost scores. Then they erupt in frustration as Bulgaria scores a second time.

A third goal for Bulgaria, and they raise their hands in disgust.

A fourth, and some start to pack up.

A column of frowning Greeks turn up the cement steps and pass by, taking their face paint and flag capes to the exits. Then I spot a trickle of Bulgarians across the stadium who are descending through all the blue and white. Just a slender thread of green and red and white.

The final whistle blows, and that colorful thread unspools over a brick wall, spilling onto the field. They run as a line toward the victorious team, clapping and pogo-jumping and chanting as they form a circle of celebration.

In the middle of them all, what else but three or four Brazilians in green-and-yellow jerseys, banging on drums. Apparently, any soccer celebration equals party time!

1990: I am back in Ethiopia, where I first learned to play this globe-spanning game, and it's 11 PM. The streets of Addis Ababa are weirdly quiet, emptied by a government curfew. In the hardline Marxist state imposed by Colonel Mengistu, people have learned to whisper because who knows who might be listening, ready to cart you off.

Nevertheless, at 11 PM, there is a sudden burst of shouting beyond the walls of the old whitewashed adobe guesthouse where I am staying.

I flip off the lights and cautiously pull back my second-story curtain. I see no one on the street, but the shouts increase. Then I am startled by a car horn, and then another, until there is a whole cacophony of horns blaring, near and far.

What is causing such alarm? Should I be sheltering in the basement of the building? Should I hide in the closet?

As I listen more closely, I realize that the shouts are not angry. What I am hearing, it seems, is not an alarm but a happy outcry. A massive citywide celebration!

Someone whoops in our hallway, so I open my door and poke my head out. "What's going on?" I ask, amazed to see a seventy-year-old British missionary in checkered pajamas, hands in the air, silver hair aswirl.

"Cameroon won!" he barks. "For the first time ever, an African team is going to the quarterfinals."

Only later will I learn about the winning goal by Roger Milla—the oldest man to play in a World Cup. I will hear the awed description of him stealing the ball from a not-quite-vigilant Colombian goalie, then pounding it into the net. But the exultation out there on the darkened streets—all the joy spilling into those sad, quiet streets—is what rises to the top of my memory.

Cameroon, on the western coast of Africa, is two thousand miles from Ethiopia. Yet what shared exultation. What continent-spanning goodwill. What refusal to stay quiet even in the middle of tyranny!

DID YOU KNOW?
Random (but Fun) Facts

The longest goal scored in competitive professional soccer was 105 yards kicked by Thomas King, the goalie for Newport County, at a 2021 game in England.

In 1996, the Brazilian soccer player Claudia Martini, one of the standout players of her time, juggled a ball for 7 hours 5 minutes 25 seconds without letting it touch the ground.

The most goals scored in any World Cup game, male or female, were by the US women's team, which defeated Thailand 13–0 in the 2019 tournament.

Goalkeeper Rogério Ceni was the designated penalty- and free-kick specialist for his team in Brazil, and he scored 131 goals during his twenty-five-year career, the most by any professional goalie.

Saudi player Nawaf Al-Abed, playing in the Prince Faisal bin Fahad Cup match, noticed that the opposing goalkeeper was too far forward at the opening kickoff, so he simply shot the ball from the center line, scoring the quickest goal ever: 2.4 seconds.

Ever think about how far refs run? In the English Premier League, they are required to stay within twenty yards of the ball, which means running as much as six to eight miles per game.

26
Camaraderie

I don't play only soccer. I also play basketball. In fact, my basketball playing goes back almost as far as soccer, having started with organized practices in seventh grade.

I'm not a great shooter, but I dribble and pass well, so I tend to play point guard. I also steal the ball well, getting it back into my team's hands. For me, the most enjoyable games are the ones when all five players become a united front, passing liberally, setting picks for each other, switching defensive assignments if an opponent breaks loose, and scoring by faking a shot, then dishing the ball to someone more open.

Basketball can be a lot of fun especially when that sort of team spirit takes over. However, the relational dynamic—even with pickup games—is generally not as warm or generous as in soccer. Over the last fifty years, I've played basketball with groups at half-a-dozen colleges, at local YMCAs, in a rented grade school gym, and so on, but I find that even when the group has years of shared experience, there is a kind of cooled-down individualism that becomes apparent from the moment we begin warming up.

If we talk, it is quiet and brief. Players move around in their own bubbles, shooting at the basket and expecting the ball to be slapped back as long as it goes through the hoop. Others wait under the basket until a missed shot, then they take that ball, dribble it to the 3-point perimeter, turn, and fire away, usually without a word.

I fall into the same stance once I'm on the court. I might throw out a greeting or make a teasing comment. But generally, I feel subdued. By contrast, when I show up at a pickup soccer game, I can expect a pleasant interchange with players sitting on the sidelines, lacing up shoes. During our prep and during warmup passing, there's a lot of chatter. And that camaraderie is not limited to just one or two exceptional groups that I have known. Even now, when I am the old fart who could be father to half of the players, I am likely to receive a series of friendly comments as I get ready to play: "Hey, didn't see you last week. Your ankle still giving you trouble? Didn't expect such a turnout, what with the low temperature. Where's your sweats? Man, you need to buy some sweats."

With pickup soccer, I also find that there is less overt conflict, at least for me. And I think this is tied to the way basketball is typically played—in a man-to-man fashion.

I grew up playing basketball in two distinctly different manners: either zone or man-to-man. With zone, everyone was quite aware of everyone else on the team, working as a coordinated unit. We kept adjusting to where the ball moved, either applying pressure or pulling back into an assigned zone until the ball shifted to our area again. Man-to-man, by contrast, turned me and my teammates into relatively independent individuals, each of us dealing with one independent entity on the opposing team. Those assigned one-on-one pairings were personal and continual, and they were potentially volatile.

Cut to the present, when man-to-man is the unwritten norm for almost all pickup basketball. Because players are constantly paired in such an individualistic fashion, heated comments are bound to break out, escalating toward pushing or worse. I'll admit that I've had dozens of arguments on basketball courts, which is not a point of pride. By contrast, though, I have had very few open aggrievements on soccer fields.

It's odd, really, how basketball brings me to a quick boil. I would see it as simply a personal weakness except that I've noticed the same phenomenon in other players. I've witnessed a lot more shouting matches between basketball players than soccer players. And even though man-to-man defense heightens the likelihood of conflict, no one seems to think of switching to the old-fashioned zone approach that we employed in my youth.

The only time I remember trying out a zone defense during an adult pickup game was when I was about thirty and my two brothers and I quietly consulted with two other players, getting them to agree to give it a go, just for fun. That's exactly what it was—fun—because the other team was immediately disoriented, becoming frustrated as their one-on-one attacks were not received in the expected manner, instead being turned over to new defenders in different areas of the court. We won the game handily even though we were no more talented. We had just changed the paradigm on them—played in a more connected manner too.

By making such comparisons, I don't mean to say that soccer players are better team players than basketball players. The same way that you can have a ball hog on a basketball court, you can have one on the soccer field. You can also have a clique of players who pass only to each other, or a defense that doesn't know how to coordinate offside traps.

However, I *do* believe that there is something especially collegial about soccer. Why? Partly because it involves more players, not locking them into noticeable one-on-one matchups with magnified tensions. Also because soccer is played in the open, where all the energy and sound dissipate rather than being bottled up. In fact, the larger space literally allows players to move more freely.

But some of that soccer-playing collegiality, I believe, is because the players are simply conditioned to think communally. Granted, good basketball players know the importance of working together, passing liberally and switching defensive assignments when they have been outrun or blocked. They huddle to agree on what happens next. They yell encouragement. But by being limited to five at a time and usually being focused on a single opponent, they are quite naturally made to think more independently, feeling the spotlight shine on them in an individualistic way.

Soccer players, due to being part of a larger, eleven-man team, are less likely to think of themselves in a solo fashion. And because of the international nature of the game, I believe they have had more practice getting along in a diverse community.

That's a bold assertion, I know, but take a close look. Although basketball has been expanding rapidly in the last twenty or thirty years, soccer is shared by virtually all nations on the globe. You can play it wherever there is a flat patch of ground, even if the goals have to be a pair of shoes spaced five feet apart. And no single nation has dominated soccer as a result—unlike basketball, which the US has ruled until recently, winning all but four of the gold medals awarded since the 1936 Olympics. With soccer, by contrast, eighteen different nations have won gold, suggesting a kind of international equity.

Hooligans aside, most soccer players and fans are aware of that long legacy of worldwide competition and multinational excellence. Whether professional or amateur, players are more prone to accept and welcome teammates or opponents who are culturally different. And the fans, though fiercely devoted to their own teams, are more likely to have a foundational respect for a wide, culturally diverse range of players and teams. Exceptions exist, particularly where there has been extreme political antipathy. But the general result is a warmer, more receptive attitude.

Need further proof? What other sport can you think of that, at the highest level possible, has players enter the arena led by children who hold their hands? And what other sport regularly promotes games called, of all things, "friendlies"?

27
No Matter What!

On June 22, 2019, a professional Ethiopian soccer team named Wollaitta Dicha tied another Ethiopian team, Bahir Dar Kenema, in a tightly contested match at Bahir Dar International Stadium, a short walk from Lake Tana, source of the Blue Nile. I know because I was there. What I *didn't* know was that in the same city, as the game began, a disgruntled former general brought a hit squad into a government meeting to assassinate the regional president. I had no idea that as my wife and I watched the game unfold, the attack was already occurring.

Our actual reason for coming to Bahir Dar was to visit medieval orthodox monasteries scattered across twenty-seven islands on Lake Tana. Having lived in Ethiopia as a youth, I had heard about the ancient adobe structures and their colorful murals featuring saints unique to the region, such as a group of monks saved from a monstrous fish by a spear-carrying angel. I also knew that many Ethiopians believed the area to be sacred because, according to legend, the Ark of the Covenant had been brought to Lake Tana in the tenth century BC by Prince Menelik, son of King Solomon and the Queen of Sheba.

History was our aim. However, when I saw Bahir Dar International Stadium next to the hotel and learned that two regional teams would square off, I insisted that we had to attend, especially since one of the teams was from the region where I had lived as a kid, 150 miles south of the Ethiopian capital. Being a good sport, Cathleen agreed, and we joined the throng walking to the stadium, which loomed higher as we approached. I didn't know that this was the newest and largest stadium in Ethiopia, but as we got close, I became intimidated by its sheer size. The hulking concrete rim blocked out the sun as we squeezed into the shadows with a boisterous crowd.

By then, I believe, the fateful cabinet meeting had started across town. Perhaps they were talking about benign things like a road-improvement initiative that would convert some city streets from gravel to asphalt. Or maybe they were getting into an argument about a proposal that the disgruntled former general had brought to the table. He was clearly tired of being ignored, wanting to matter the way he had mattered before he was jailed by a previous regime. I imagine him ranting about how the northwestern region of Ethiopia had once been the pride of the nation, seat of the famous emperor Tewodros—who, in his opinion, had twice the balls of any current politician.

All that is speculation, though. In reality, when we reached the stadium gate, guarded by soldiers with rifles, I had no inkling of the impending trouble. I was simply trying to convince Cathleen that she should not worry about us being the only foreign faces in a sea of Ethiopians or her being one of only four or five women—something that, in retrospect, I treated too lightly.

The guards, doubling as ticket agents, indicated that we should have purchased our tickets back in the direction from which we had come. However, when they saw our hapless confusion, they waved us through. With all the press of people, we had little choice anyway, so we joined the compressed column of fans and shuffled through an unlit, echoing corridor. Then we emerged, blinking, into blazing sunlight.

After my vision adjusted, I could see that the interior of Bahir Dar International Stadium was a gigantic ringed oval capable of seating sixty thousand, and it looked as if it had just been poured yesterday—as if an immense mold had been lifted off the monolith that very morning. There were no seats, only bench-like shelves stairstepping higher and higher. There were no glassed-in booths for VIPs or press reporters, no awnings, no lights, no signs, no paint even. Just a half-mile loop of concrete rings with a lined running track down at the bottom of the crater and, inside that, a grassy field where two teams were batting balls around, warming up.

Maybe it was the immensity of the space, but when I scanned the swarming crowd at this stadium, I was reminded of Meskel Square at the heart of Addis Ababa, where runners used to compete when I was a child and where major events would be hosted, including a huge bonfire on Meskel Day, which commemorates the crucifixion of Christ. In the 1970s, after Emperor Selassie was overthrown and sixty parliamentary leaders were forced against a wall and shot, that square was renamed Revolution Square and three huge billboards were erected, depicting Marx, Engels, and Lenin. People still gathered, but they came because they were forced to march in support of the revolution.

"Death to the imperialists, death to America," Colonel Mengistu shouted at one of those required rallies. Then he lifted a bottle of blood and smashed it on his podium. I know because I was on a bus that afternoon traveling into Addis with my father, and we had to listen as his strident voice crackled out of the bus sound system, noting that other passengers would not meet our gaze anymore.

Having just been back to Addis with Cathleen and having passed by that public square, I was still in the grip of a strange déjà vu. Forty years had passed since Mengistu's "Red Terror," yet I could hardly believe that athletes were now running drills up and down the stone bleachers, as they had when I was young, or that soccer goals stood where Mengistu had screamed, "Death to America."

Clearly, this was no longer the Ethiopia of the Marxist revolution, neither in Addis Ababa nor in this regional capital. Nonetheless, as Cathleen and I stood in the massive Bahir Dar Stadium, surrounded by loudly talking Ethiopians, I felt an old anxiety throw a shadow over me. I was very aware that we were drawing attention, so I led Cathleen up the cement risers to an empty space, and we scooched back against the next step, sitting cross-legged. Quickly, others filled in around us, and a row of teenage boys plunked onto the concrete shelf below us, turning to ask in broken English, "Hello, how ar-ra you? What country are you from? Do you like it here? Which team are you wanting?"

They were surprised that I spoke a bit of Amharic, at least enough to say I only knew a little—"Bizu Amarinya alawik'imi." They were even more surprised when I said that as a child, I had lived in Wolaita—the region of the opposing team. They couldn't believe I knew the capital of Wolaita, which is Sodo. Eager now, they asked whether I was cheering for the visiting team, but I shook my head diplomatically, saying I would be happy whoever won—that I was just glad to see a game played in the country I had known as a child.

These teens were very persistent. Eventually, the most aggressive jumped up and sat right next to Cathleen, which amused the others and made him more brash. "How is life in America?" he demanded. "How can I come?" Then the game began, which gave us a reprieve from his string of questions.

It was not a very compelling game, to be honest, although we saw a lot of good ball control. Ethiopian players tend to be slighter than most African players and therefore depend more on footwork finesse than muscular play. In villages, kids love to outfox opponents, and they get hoots of praise if they show dribbling prowess.

In any case, no one was taking major chances, instead just trying to maintain ball control . . . until at last a Bahir Dar player was tripped in the penalty area, which resulted in a successful penalty kick. The stadium broke into a wild fit of cheering. You could see the local pride shining, and the teens in front of us, while yelling victoriously, glanced back at me with wry grins.

After another twenty minutes, a breakaway striker from Wollaitta got loose long enough to take an open shot and tie the game, causing a round of Amharic curses and hands thrown in the air. However, I don't remember much else about the action on the field, in part because I was so conscious of the boys swiveling to quiz us. Cathleen, in a generous attempt to be friendly, had shared peanuts and a bag of candy from a vendor who wandered by, which meant the group became more interactive rather than less, and I was struggling—with poor hearing—to understand even half of what they were saying.

As much as we might want to blend in, we couldn't escape our foreignness, which felt magnified by the fact that Cathleen really was the only female in our section of the stands. I was still glad to participate in this slice of Ethiopian life and glad that Cathleen was joining me outside her comfort zone. However, sitting in that crowd was raising more stress than expected.

What was happening in the cabinet meeting by then? I can only guess. Had the hit squad come into the room? Had they fired the fatal shots, killing the regional president and his aide? Or would that happen later, after we stepped back into our hotel?

I will never know such specifics. But I do remember that after the game ended in a 1–1 tie and after we had reached our room at last, to rest before supper, we received an odd text from family friends who had hosted us in Addis before we made this side strip. Burakie asked, "Are you okay?"

"Yes," I tapped into a phone he had lent us. "Doing great. Just went to a Bahir Dar soccer game."

"Are you sure it is safe?"

"A big crowd, but we are fine."

"Maybe be more careful."

I looked at Cathleen. "What's he so worried about?"

"I suppose crowds could have a bad reputation here?" she theorized. "Maybe fighting happens? Or maybe he just knows you shouldn't be taking your wife into a stadium with so many men!"

I smirked in acknowledgment of her sardonic jab.

"We will be careful," I tapped into the phone, wanting to allay further fears. Then we went down to supper, and for the first time we got an actual clue about what had made him cautionary. The TV was turned on in the dining room, and the staff kept stopping to stare at it, almost forgetting to take orders. On the screen, sad music played and photos of two men kept appearing with lit candles. The somber announcer spoke Amharic, and I recognized a few words. Then we surmised from his tone and the wistful distraction of the staff that somebody important must have died.

Our waiter tried to deflect my first question, saying, "There is nothing to worry about. Just some troubles. Everything will be better tomorrow."

"But who died?"

He hesitated. However, seeing my determination, he admitted, "A leader here has been killed. But not to worry. They have found the people who did this. They have captured them."

Only after dinner, when we went to the check-in desk and asked deliberate questions, did we piece together a more complete picture. Not only had the regional president been assassinated right here in Bahir Dar, but the perpetrator had fought an extended gun battle, resisting until shot and killed. Then, in retaliation, a government bodyguard in Addis Ababa who was loyal to the dead rebel had suddenly turned his gun on the Ethiopian secretary of defense, slaying *him*. What had started as a local issue had turned into a national crisis.

By the next morning, the entire country had gone dark. No

more TV broadcasts. No working ATMs. No cell service. No Wi-Fi to send an email. Nothing.

"Not to worry," the hotel manager insisted at the front desk, but the last text we had received from our friends in Addis had asked urgently, "Maybe return here now?"

Cathleen and I deliberated for an hour or two, not sure what to do. As we pondered the problem, we sat on a verandah five or six stories above the streets of Bahir Dar, gazing down at a large park with a cement play area. Little Asian tuk-tuks scuttled down side streets, taxiing people to work or to shops. A man quick-walked past the hotel gate with a bundle of iron rebar on his shoulder. An elderly woman in a black headscarf paused under eucalyptus trees to talk to a friend who held the hand of a patient girl, and that girl stared toward the park, where two teams of boys chased a worn brown soccer ball that looked more plastic than leather.

Even from up there on the verandah, I could tell that those soccer-playing kids, dashing around their ad hoc concrete soccer pitch, were totally invested in the game. Back and forth they stampeded between goals that were indicated by two piles of rock, competing just as other children had done when I was their age and Emperor Selassie was on the throne or when Colonel Mengistu wrenched away political control or when the army of the Tigre resistance movement ousted Mengistu, who jumped aboard a plane and fled to Zimbabwe.

The ball skipped across the concrete, having no grass to slow it. The boys—in ragged tennis shoes or sandals—raced after it. And we sat in silence, weighing options.

I knew that if we went to the airport to try to leave Bahir Dar, all flights would be booked, crammed with government officials and anxious travelers who had acted more quickly than we had. Buses would be jammed too, and they seemed more vulnerable, requiring up to ten hours of bumping through territory that could erupt any moment if this situation was as dangerous as our friends in Addis seemed to think.

A tuk-tuk honked at the gate to the hotel, and the guard swung it open. The children on one of the soccer teams shouted triumphantly as the ball skipped between the stacks of rocks. The sun beat down. The world kept turning. And I suddenly said to Cathleen, "Look out there. Does it seem like war breaking out?"

She gave me a raised eyebrow, and I continued, "For now, I think we should just stay in Bahir Dar, where it seems relatively safe. In fact, I think we should do what we originally planned, taking one of those boats out onto the lake to see monasteries."

She wasn't as sure. However, she hadn't lived through an actual revolution, as I had. She hadn't crossed Addis Ababa week after week in a bus full of soccer teammates, stopped every mile or two at checkpoints that were manned by neighborhood police with AK-47s. For good or ill, she trusted me, so we went down to the bottom floor and crossed the courtyard of the hotel, then stepped through the little pedestrian door in the larger auto gate.

As we skirted the concrete play area, we stopped to watch the children with their plastic soccer ball. They were still playing as if nothing existed except that scuffed orb—as if there had been no assassinations, as if the game would keep going long after all the generals in the world had made their demands and learned that they were not actually in charge.

When we were finally ready to ride to the lake, we waved down one of the three-wheeled tuk-tuks, haggled over the price, and climbed into the little compartment behind the driver.

"Welcome to Bahir Dar," he said.

Then he swung the handlebars, gunned the engine, and took off toward a future that would be what it would be.

DID YOU KNOW?

Who Outlasted All the Others?

Stanley Matthews, who played his last professional game in 1965, is considered one of England's greatest soccer players, and until recently, he was the oldest professional soccer player to stay active, playing until he was fifty. However, Matthews has finally been passed by Japan's Kazuyoshi Miura, who is still playing and currently on loan to the Portuguese club Oliveirense at fifty-six years old.

Miura, known affectionately as Kazu, started his career in 1986, and he was the first Japanese player to receive the Asian Player of the Year award in 1993. He has scored 218 total goals, and in 2022, while playing for the Suzuka Point Getters, he became the oldest player to score a competitive goal, getting the ball into the net twice at the age of fifty-five.

As for Stanley Matthews, England's oldest, after he retired, he coached soccer in South Africa, and in 1975, he established an all-Black team in Soweto, resisting the country's apartheid laws. He is, to this day, the only soccer player to be knighted for services to football.

28

The Old Man and the Knee

My wife smiles as I come up from the laundry room with my soccer gear. The smile is one of those isn't-he-cute-but-a-bit-out-of-touch smirks, and it is usually accompanied by a witty comment about me looking like an aging medieval knight preparing for his last battle—perhaps King Théoden from *The Lord of the Rings* strapping on a leather breastplate.

I'm not amused, so I frown as I pull on my knee brace and add a neoprene sleeve around a strained hamstring. I don't give her the benefit of a retort as I tape my left ankle, then lie on the floor pretzeling my legs to loosen a stiff back. I'm not willing to see myself as silly yet, even though I know she's got a point.

Don Quixote has nothing on me, so why in the hell do I keep doing this? Sheer habit? Addiction? Or could it be something more primal—a life force, of sorts, that refuses the limits of age until death has its way?

When I was twentysomething, there wasn't all this preparatory ritual. I yanked on shorts and jumped into the game. I'm not sure I even stretched. Not until I hit thirty did I have an athletic limitation worse than a pulled groin. Then I partially tore the ACL in my left knee, so I could no longer lunge and extend my other leg to snag the ball from a veering attacker.

It's been an uphill battle ever since. Here's the deal: each year as I get older and more decrepit, a new cadre of young men and women join the ranks of those I play against. They are college kids who can sprint and shove and shoot like college kids. It's getting tough to last a full game on the same field, and the compliments tend to be harder-earned, backed by an unspoken "Not bad for an old guy."

Yet I keep strapping on the knee brace and stretching aching joints, and I suppose that is because being able to compete even at an average level makes me feel validated somehow. To perform at all—not goofing so badly that I must leave the field of honor—is to feel secretly reassured that I still "have it," whatever "it" is. And if I actually outplay one of those younger athletes? Oh, what bliss.

These days, I will use any strategy that might give me an edge. I even use my age sometimes. For instance, if I am being chased down the sideline by a galloping youth, I might glance to the center of the field as if desperate for help. I might also bring my outer foot back and swing it sharply, wanting to appear as if I am making a long, frantic pass. But instead of kicking the ball, at the last instant, I will plant my inner foot, bringing my body to a halt, and I will stop the swinging foot so that I can hook the ball and pull it back. The defender, who is much faster than I am and all stretched out to block an imagined pass, will fly by if all goes well, and that means I am left standing alone, able to dribble to the middle of the field.

There are surprised hoots of delight on such occasions, and I'll admit it: I love that hubbub. The twenty-year-olds don't expect this from me. They laugh and shout. Afterward, they bump fists with me. They are greatly amused to see the eagerness of a guy their own age being foiled by an older, slower guy with gray hair and twenty pounds of extra belly fat.

Which makes me think, paradoxically, of a time when I might have been considered one of the younger guys, playing on a team that dominated the thirty-plus league in Manhattan, Kansas. Our goalbox was rarely challenged back then. In fact, it was so safe that we decided one day to let my aging father play keeper just for fun. I remember vividly the moment when an opponent finally broke through our defensive line and fired off a line drive. Dad had no experience with soccer, but he instinctively threw himself to the side, not able to leap so much as fall, and his fingertips sent the ball wide, skittering around the post. A perfect save!

That afternoon, the guys on my team hoisted him onto their shoulders in an impromptu parade. My brother Nat and Jorge and Mustapha and Siendou held him high, cheering wildly, and he laughed so hard that he cried. He laughed, yes, but he also shone.

My father was pushing seventy by then, and though I'm still in my mid-sixties, I understand now why Dad risked diving after that ball and why he laughed so happily. When I hit his age, I hope I'll have such a moment too. Just one more moment of being lifted toward the sun. And then, who knows, maybe one more . . .

Acknowledgments

First, thanks to Editor in Chief Joyce Harrison, who believed in my writing and said yes. And thanks to the team at University Press of Kansas, who turned the words into a physical book, getting it onto your shelf.

Thanks also to fellow authors who helped me hone the language and structure, particularly Tom Averill and Andrew Milward. And many, many thanks to my lit-savvy wife, who is skilled not only as a writer but also as a reader. Cathleen, this book would not be what it is without your keen observations and encouragement!

Thanks as well to my sons, Luke and Conrad, for sharing a love of the game, whether playing or watching. And finally, thanks to all the soccer players who have welcomed me onto the field, especially those who have been an inspiration in recent years: Oumar, Erika, Song, Oscar, Julio, Mike, Will, Xin Kai, and my brother Nat, who has been a faithful and fun soccer-playing companion for half a century!